CHESS NOT CHECKERS

Other books by the author:

The Heart of Leadership

The Secret of Teams

The Secret *with Ken Blanchard*

Great Leaders Grow *with Ken Blanchard*

Field Guides:

Chess Not Checkers

The Heart of Leadership

The Secret of Teams

THE HIGH-PERFORMANCE SERIES

CHESS NOT CHECKERS

ELEVATE YOUR LEADERSHIP GAME

MARK MILLER

BK°

Berrett–Koehler Publishers, Inc.

Berrett-Koehler Publishers, Inc.
1333 Broadway, Suite 1000
Oakland, CA 94612-1921
Tel: (510) 817-2277   Fax: (510) 817-2278   www.bkconnection.com

Ordering Information

Quantity sales. Special discounts are available on quantity purchases by corporations, associations, and others. For details, contact the "Special Sales Department" at the Berrett-Koehler address above.

Individual sales. Berrett-Koehler publications are available through most bookstores. They can also be ordered directly from Berrett-Koehler:
Tel: (800) 929-2929; Fax: (802) 864-7626; www.bkconnection.com

Orders for college textbook/course adoption use. Please contact Berrett-Koehler: Tel: (800) 929-2929; Fax: (802) 864-7626.

Distributed to the U.S. trade and internationally by Penguin Random House Publisher Services.

Berrett-Koehler and the BK logo are registered trademarks of Berrett-Koehler Publishers, Inc.

Printed in the United States of America

Berrett-Koehler books are printed on long-lasting acid-free paper. When it is available, we choose paper that has been manufactured by environmentally responsible processes. These may include using trees grown in sustainable forests, incorporating recycled paper, minimizing chlorine in bleaching, or recycling the energy produced at the paper mill.

Library of Congress Cataloging-in-Publication Data
Miller, Mark, 1959–
      Chess not checkers : elevate your leadership game / Mark Miller. —
            pages   cm.—(A BK business book)
      ISBN 978-1-62656-394-0 (hardcover)
      1.Leadership. 2. Management. 3. Strategic planning. I. Title.
      HD57.7.M5373 2015
      658.4'092—dc23
                                                                            2014041025

First Edition
25   24   23   22   21   20   19   10   9   8   7   6   5   4

Production Management: Michael Bass Associates
Cover Design: Irene Morris
Chess Piece: TheChessStore.com

This book is dedicated to Truett Cathy. It was my privilege to watch and learn from him for almost four decades as he created his own high performance organization.

Contents

Introduction

Leading has never been easy. From our first exper-iment trying to get our classmates to follow us or receiving our first official assignment at work, leader-ship has always demanded our best effort. That hasn't changed—but something else has: the complexity of the problems we face and the organizations we lead has increased exponentially.

Perhaps this complexity finds its energy in the scope of your enterprise, or it may merely be a function of increased volume. These are great problems to have ... if leaders can orchestrate an appropriate response.

Unfortunately, for many leaders, our past suc-cesses just don't translate. The game has literally changed before our eyes. The methods that worked extremely well in the past no longer have the same effect. In many cases, the tried and true has become the tired and tarnished.

Most of us began our leadership journey utilizing an approach with striking similarities to the game of checkers, a fun, highly reactionary game often played at a frantic pace. Any strategies we employed in this style of leadership were limited, if not rudimentary.

The opportunities in our world for leaders to play checkers and be successful are dwindling.

The game today for most leaders can better be compared to chess—a game in which strategy matters; a game in which individual pieces have unique abilities that drive unique contributions; a game in which heightened focus and a deeper level of thinking are required to win.

Although *Chess Not Checkers* provides a rich metaphor for leaders, it is much more than that. The game of chess contains four specific parallels that can inform and transform any organization seeking new levels of performance. I've positioned each of these ideas as a "move" your organization can make to draw closer to your goals. Collectively, these moves can be your blueprint for sustained high performance.

I hope this simple story will resonate with you. The company Blake leads is not real, although the situations he faces are as relevant as today's news. I've intentionally omitted details about his organization, leaving it largely nameless and faceless. Hopefully, this approach will make it easier for you to think about your own organization. Is it possible you may be playing checkers when the game is chess? If that is your situation, today can be the day you start learning a new game.

It's your move!

The Decision

*If you miss the "opportunity of a lifetime,"
do you ever get another one?*

Blake wrote these words in his journal, put down his
pen, and stared out the kitchen window. He had got-
ten up early; he couldn't sleep, anyway. His mind was
racing as he reflected on his life and career up until
this point.

The last decade had been a whirlwind. After his
father died, Blake had invested five years trying to live
up to his dad's expectations. Jeff had always believed
his son could lead. Blake had never been sure, but he
pushed through his doubts and dedicated himself to
learning the skills of leadership.

Blake's leadership journey had been frustrating.
After learning to cast vision, build teams, get results,
and more, he had been passed over for formal leadership positions. Confused by this turn of events, he
reached out to his longtime mentor, Debbie Brewster.
She helped him gain the greatest insight of his life thus
far: *If your heart is not right, no one cares about your skills.*

This revelation led Blake to the next phase in his journey. Armed with the skills he had learned, he began working diligently to strengthen his leadership character. According to those closest to Blake, it was working. Blake was becoming a leader people wanted to follow.

Now, a decade into his career, he finally felt like he understood leadership. The men and women he worked with seemed to agree. There were rumors Blake might someday move into senior leadership. But still, Blake was skeptical about his future at Dynastar, and he had lingering doubts about his own leadership. If he had so much potential, why hadn't he already been given a position of leadership? All these thoughts made Blake's current decision even more difficult.

The options were clear: stay at Dynastar with the *hope* of a bright future, or take an offer to be the CEO of a small business in a nearby community.

"Small" was a relative term. The business had annual sales of several million dollars and employed more than fifty people. Blake's income would be more than he was currently making, but that was not what excited him. Based on what he had learned, he believed the business had tremendous untapped potential. He was convinced that in a few years, he could double the sales—and profits. The upside opportunity was significant.

There were still two lingering issues. The flat sales had not escaped the notice of the parent company. They were eager for a turnaround. In his conversations with senior leaders, Blake had the distinct impression he would need to make things happen quickly or the business could be closed or sold. His challenge would be to get it back on a growth trajectory as quickly as possible.

The other issue was Megan. Happily married to Blake for just over ten years, she had been with him every step of the way. Blake knew she was unsure about him making this move.

Blake went to the counter to get another cup of coffee as Megan came into the kitchen. "Good morning," he said.

"Morning," Megan mumbled as she made her way to the coffee maker. Blake handed her a cup, and she cradled it with both hands and held her face six inches over the cup to breathe in the warmth. Now somewhat awake, she said, "Today's the day you need to make a decision, isn't it?"

"Yes, it is."

"Have you decided?"

"I'm going to do it."

"What tipped the scales?" Megan asked.

"I see this as a huge opportunity for us. It looks to me like the business has been over-managed and under-led."

"You know you have my full support, and I hate to mention it, but I have one last question," Megan said reluctantly.

"Okay." Blake leaned forward.

"You have never led a company." She looked at him lovingly, "Do you know how?"

"I think so," Blake confessed.

"Your confidence overwhelms me," she smiled.

It looks to me like the business has been over-managed and under-led.

"Well, you're right—I have never led a company. However, I do know a lot about leadership. That's what I've been doing the last decade—learning to lead."

"Yes, I know, and I can see, even here at home, you are a much better leader than you were then. But leading a cross-functional team and leading a multimillion-dollar organization seem," she paused, "well, different."

"I've thought about that, and I agree—but I believe I can figure it out."

"Okay," Megan gave a forced smile.

"With your support, I know this can be a good change for us," Blake said, sensing her hesitation.

"I'm all in." She reached across the table and grabbed his hand.

"Me, too! I'll make the call this morning."

Harder Than It Looks

Blake made the call and signed the papers. He went to his boss at Dynastar and announced his decision. Then he told his teammates. He shared that he had stumbled on the opportunity of a lifetime and felt like he needed to give it a try. All these conversations went surprisingly well, and everyone was extremely encouraging.

On Monday morning, Blake drove to his new company. He arrived early—early enough to be the first one there. With a little convincing, a security guard finally let him in since Blake didn't have keys yet.

While waiting for the day to officially begin, he sat at his desk and stared at his new laptop. Just as he realized he didn't know the password, his thoughts were interrupted by a knock.

"Good morning, sir. I'm Suzy, your assistant." She stopped and then added, "Or I hope I will be." Her voice trailed off.

A middle-aged Asian woman, Suzy was wearing a long-sleeved T-shirt, handmade beaded necklace, and sweat pants; she finished off her ensemble with large glasses with bright red frames. She was clearly underdressed for the office by Blake's standards. However, he chose not to say anything about her appearance on their first meeting.

"Come in, Suzy. Have a seat. Can you repeat what you just said? I didn't quite hear you."

"I said I'm your assistant." She paused.

"Yes, I heard that, but did you say something about hope?"

"Yes," she looked at the floor and fidgeted with a file folder in her hand as she spoke. "I said I hope I'll be your assistant."

"What does that mean?" Blake was puzzled.

"Well, sir, I was the former CEO's assistant, but HR has warned us all we may not have a job after you arrive."

"Why would they say that?"

"I guess you'll have to ask them."

"Okay, I will, but why do you think they would say that?"

"I assume ... it might be because our performance needs to improve, and to improve performance, you'll have to make changes. Or ... maybe it's because the last CEO fired several people on his first day."

"Really?"

"Yes, sir."

"I don't want people to be fearful they might lose their jobs—but it sounds like it's too late for that."

"Yes, sir, I'm afraid it is. So, am I still your assistant?"

"Of course."

"Outstanding!" Suzy flashed a huge smile of relief.

"How can I help?"

"I'd love to know what you did to serve the previous CEO."

"I did whatever he asked me to do."

Blake was waiting for Suzy to continue, but she was obviously finished.

"Okay, we will want to talk more about that later. For now, can you help me with my password?"

"Yes, it's THE_MAN, in all caps."

"You're kidding."

"No, sir."

"Okay, we'll want to change that."

"Yes, sir. As soon as someone from IT gets here this morning, I'll make sure it's done. What do you want it to be?"

"I don't care. Something simple."

"Okay, when you decide, let me know." Suzy turned and walked away.

Blake started to call her back to resolve the issue but decided to wait until later. For now, he wanted to quickly check his email before his first meeting.

He typed in THE_MAN and when his email opened, he was shocked. He had over two hundred messages. Quickly scrolling through them, he noticed at least 25 percent had the words *Decision Needed* in the subject line. He knew this was going to take some time and focus, so he shut down his computer and asked Suzy to give him a quick tour of the facility and show him the conference room where he would meet his executive team.

As they walked, Blake noticed the place looked cluttered. There were boxes everywhere, and most of the desks had piles of file folders and papers on them. Blake also realized no one was at work even though it was now approaching 8:45.

When Blake asked Suzy about this, she said, "We start slow around here. Today, since it's Monday, most people will probably be in by 9:15."

Blake thought that was odd, but once again didn't say anything.

When they arrived at the meeting room, Blake said, "Thanks for the tour. When you get back to your office, please start going through my email for me and do what you can with it."

"I'm sorry, sir, I'm not comfortable doing that."

Blake, a little frustrated, said, "Okay, we can discuss it after this meeting."

At 9:00, the scheduled start time, only three of the five invitees were present: John Roberts, Vice President of Marketing; Angie Stevens, Vice President of Purchasing; and Brad Montgomery, Vice President of Finance.

Blake met each one at the door as they arrived and introduced himself. As everyone took their seats, he asked, "Who's not here who would typically be in a meeting like this?"

The three looked at him and one another. Initially, no one said anything. Then, finally, Angie raised her hand. "Yes, Angie, and you don't have to raise your hand. Who's not here who should be?"

"Well, Mr. Brown, . . . "

Blake interrupted, "You can call me Blake."

"Okay, Blake. It's kind of hard to answer your question."

"Why is that?"

"I'm assuming you invited Charles and Elizabeth, but I'm not sure. And, when you say 'typically at a meeting like this'—there's nothing typical about this meeting."

"What do you mean?"

"We don't meet," Brad said.

"Okay, that's fine." As Blake was contemplating a further response, a middle-aged woman wearing jeans and a sweatshirt stepped into the room.

"You must be Elizabeth. I'm Blake. Nice to meet you."

"Sorry I'm late. I'm not used to starting my days so early." She smiled at the group, and Blake noticed John and Angie nodding in agreement with her comment. He decided the best thing to do in the moment was to keep moving. Turning toward the group, Blake asked, "Anybody know if Charles is going to join us?"

"Did you send him an email?" Elizabeth asked.

"Yes, I did."

"Then he's probably not coming. He doesn't really do email. I'll be sure he gets any notes from this morning."

Blake was having some difficulty taking all this in. He hadn't been on site an hour, and he was already seeing major issues—starting with his own team.

"Thanks for taking notes for Charles. This should be a short meeting."

"Thank goodness," Brad said in a hushed tone but loud enough for everyone to hear.

Still trying to orient himself, Blake said, "I only have three objectives for this meeting: I want to get to know each of you a little better, and I want to hear about our goals and understand our challenges."

"That could be hard," Angie said.

"Why?"

"Well, we can do the get-to-know-you part and explain our challenges, but the goals ... I'm not sure what they are. Anybody else know?" She looked around the table. All she got in return were blank stares from her co-workers.

Angie added, "I think we have some; unfortunately, I believe Charles may have written those down, and he's not here."

"Okay, let me ask another question: It's June. How are we doing against our plan?"

"Our plan—what plan?" John asked.

"We really don't have one, but we have some financial data," Brad offered as a consolation.

"Great!" Blake said. "How are we doing?"

"Last month's profit and loss statement is in your inbox. So far, we are slightly behind where we were at this point last year," Brad offered in a matter-of-fact tone.

"That's why we're here. We're going to improve our performance over last year."

"And how are we going to do that?" Elizabeth asked.

"That's what we need to decide."

"We?" John was confused, and so was everyone else.

_____

I want to get to know each of you a little better, and I want to hear about our goals and understand our challenges.

_____

Elizabeth frowned and said, "That's not what we do. That's your job. You figure out what we need to do, and we do it. If it works, outstanding; if it doesn't, well, ... " her voice trailed off.

"If it doesn't work, what?" Blake decided to lean in just a little.

"Well, if history repeats itself," John began, "we'll be meeting the next CEO."

"Thank you for your candor. I need to know what you're thinking—not just today, but every day. If we are going to accomplish what I believe we can, we'll need everyone to say what's on their mind. We will talk more about our performance and our plan in future meetings. Now, let's take five minutes each to share our stories. I'll go first. . . ."

Over the next half hour, the men and women on Blake's "executive team" discovered things they had never known about each other, even though they had worked together for a long time. Elizabeth had climbed Mount Kilimanjaro, Brad was one of nine children, and Angie collected butterflies. They learned interesting bits of biographical information from everyone on the team. From Blake's perspective, it was a small victory.

After the meeting, Blake went back to his office to look at his email. When he asked Suzy for the password, she said, "Since you didn't tell me what you wanted, I chose Boss#5."

"What's that mean?" Blake asked.

"You're the fifth CEO."

"Really? This company is only ten years old."

"Ten and a half, to be precise."

"That doesn't sound healthy to me."

"Who said we were healthy?" She turned and walked out.

Blake shook his head in disbelief. He turned his chair and opened his email. As he read the messages, they fell roughly into four categories: requests for decisions, messages from the headquarters, customer complaints, and junk.

Not knowing what else to do, he started responding to the messages. To the customers with issues, he apologized and promised a quick resolution. To the requests for information from headquarters, he asked for more time. Regarding the decisions, he made the ones he could and forwarded others to his leadership team members.

Blake was feeling some sense of satisfaction as the inbox got smaller and smaller. He was so focused, he lost track of time. It was Suzy once again who broke his trance.

"Mr. Brown?"

"Call me Blake, please."

"Yes, sir, I'll try. Old habits are hard to break. Is there anything you want me to do for you before I leave?"

"Leave? Where are you going?"

"Home, sir, unless you want me to stay."

"What time is it?"

"Five o'clock."

"Seriously? I can't believe I've been sitting here all day."

"Well, sir, it's a big job, answering all those emails."

"Does this happen every day?"

"Like bats out of hell. They just keep coming. Every day it looks about the same."

"Really? How did the former CEO handle it?"

"I screened them, and he did the rest."

"Yes, yes. We talked about that this morning, and you said you weren't comfortable with that approach."

"Well, I thought we needed to talk first. You have to tell me how you want me to respond."

"Give me an example."

"Previously, I was told to delete messages from the headquarters. Is that what you want?"

"Absolutely not."

"Well, I wasn't sure. That's why I thought we should talk. Once I know what you want me to do, I'll do it."

"That's fair. Can we meet about that first thing in the morning?"

"Yes, sir. What time?"

"Let's start at 8:00."

"Yes, sir, and thanks for not firing anyone today."

"Thank you for not quitting after having five CEOs in ten years. One more thing—what's the dress code around here?"

"Dress code? I don't think we have one."

"Well, we're going to establish one. Business casual will be our standard. I'll communicate that with the leadership team. Let's you and I start tomorrow. We'll set the pace for the others."

Suzy understood Blake's message. "Yes, sir. Got it."

"Thanks for all your help today. I know this is a big job, and there is no way I could do it without you. I'm glad you're on the team. See you in the morning."

Blake stayed another half hour or so; he finished the emails he could and was able to see what Suzy had described—his inbox was growing right before his eyes. Before he left the building, he walked the floor. Everyone was gone. Not that he expected a lot of people to work into the night, but the office was a ghost town, and it was only 5:30. At Dynastar, there would have been much more activity at that time of day. All he'd observed on this first day gave him a sinking feeling—there was much to be done.

■ ■ ■

When Blake got home, Megan met him at the door. She gave him a big hug and a kiss. "Welcome home, my favorite CEO. How was it?"

Blake knew better than to try to fool her. He smiled, "It's going to be a challenge."

"Harder than you thought?"

"Probably so. I'm just used to Dynastar. And, although we weren't perfect, we were way ahead of what I saw today."

"You love a challenge."

"I guess," Blake managed a forced smile.

"What's the biggest challenge you saw today?" Megan asked.

"There were several, but the biggest may be the way we are doing the work—I think it's all wrong."

"What do you mean?"

"I don't know exactly. It seems like every decision and every problem comes to me. You should have seen some of the emails I responded to today. It's just not working. And, I'm convinced responding to urgent emails is not going to fix anything."

"What are you going to do?"

"I'm going to call Debbie. I haven't talked to her in months. She doesn't even know about my new role."

"That sounds like a good idea to me," Megan said.

Something Has to Change

Debbie Brewster was the third-most influential person in Blake's life. After his mom and dad, Debbie had invested more in him than anyone else. She taught Blake how to lead. And the irony of it all was that since Blake's late father had mentored Debbie, many of the principles she shared with him came, indirectly, from his dad.

Regarding his current challenges, Blake had complete confidence Debbie could help. He called her and she agreed to meet early the next morning. They met in the coffee shop they had used as a central meeting place on and off for a decade.

"Good morning!" Debbie said as soon as Blake walked through the door.

"Good morning to you," he said.

"How are you and Megan and the kids? We've got a lot of catching up to do," Debbie said.

In no time at all, the two friends had reconnected. After a few minutes, Debbie said, "When you called, you said you had a new job. You're a CEO now. Congratulations! How's it going?"

"Well, it looks like it's going to be really challenging," Blake confessed.

"Tell me more."

Blake took the next few minutes to share what he'd learned so far. He concluded by saying, "If I don't turn this around quickly, I'll need your help finding a new job!"

Debbie said with a smile, "Urgency is often a gift—it can create both clarity and action."

"It doesn't feel like a gift right now. What do you think I should do?"

"I don't know."

"You don't?" Blake was horrified. "If you don't know, I'm in deep trouble."

Urgency is often a gift—it can create both clarity and action.

"Blake, I've never led a large organization."

"So, where does that leave me?" Blake said.

"You'll be fine. You just need a different mentor."

"A different mentor?"

"Sure, we've talked about this before. Most of us need multiple mentors in our life. Someone who can coach, encourage, and counsel us in one arena may not be best suited to do so in another."

"Do you have someone in mind?"

"I do. You need to meet Jack Deluca."

"Great! Who is he?"

"He's a retired CEO and a friend of mine. He was very good leading large, complex organizations."

"Where does he live?"

"About two hours from here. I'll send him an email introducing you and leave the rest up to you."

"Thank you!

As promised, Debbie sent an email to Jack. The next day, Jack called Blake.

"Blake, this is Jack Deluca. Debbie Brewster suggested I call you."

"Yes, sir. Thank you!"

"How can I serve you?"

"I'm a new CEO, and I could use some help."

"Okay, I'd love to give you a hand," Jack said.

"We probably need to talk about your fee." Blake had no idea how expensive this might be.

"Here's my offer: I'll help you if you promise to pay it forward."

"Is that all? Can't I pay you?"

Jack laughed and said, "No, son, you couldn't afford me. Besides, I'm at a stage in my life when one more consulting job is of little interest to me."

"Then, if I may ask, why are you willing to help me?"

"My focus now is on helping leaders who can make a big difference in the world. Debbie tells me you are one of those leaders. Based on what she's already told me, I also believe you'll actually pay it forward. I never want to help someone who won't help others."

"Yes, sir, I will. When do we start?"

"I'm not a young man, so we should probably start soon," Jack said with a chuckle.

"How soon?"

"Are you available next Thursday morning?"

"Yes, sir."

"Meet me at Gresham Park at 10:00 a.m. Do you know where that is?"

"I'll find it. How will I find you?"

"Find the crowd; you'll find me. See you there!"

A Different Game

On Thursday morning, before Blake left his house, he did a quick Google search for Jack Deluca. He quickly learned Debbie had understated Mr. Deluca's accomplishments. He had not only led a wildly successful global organization but also served on several presidential task forces; he was a major donor to numerous universities, and he was named the most admired CEO by several magazines over three decades. All of this fueled Blake's desire to be a little bit early. He didn't think Jack was a man you wanted to keep waiting.

When Blake got to the park, he began to walk. He wasn't exactly sure what he was looking for, other than a crowd. He walked past a large playground and then he saw about twenty-five people standing around a picnic table. He couldn't see who was at the table but assumed it was Jack.

He pushed his way through the people surrounding the table to see what was going on. Two men stared at a chessboard. One man was in his early twenties; Blake recognized the other man from the media photos: Jack Deluca.

Jack appeared to be in his early 70s, fit, and well groomed. He was wearing a sweater and a wool hat. When Blake made eye contact with Jack, he offered a timid wave. Jack nodded. Then he looked across the table at the young man, smiled, made his move, and said, "Checkmate."

The man looked stunned, and the crowd began to cheer.

"Okay, ladies and gentlemen, that's all for today. I have a meeting with an important CEO. I'll see you next time."

Jack shook hands with his opponent, who still seemed a bit shocked by the game's sudden end.

As the people began to disperse, Jack turned to Blake and said, "Jack Deluca's my name. Glad to meet you." As he extended his hand, he said, "Have a seat."

Blake sat down, still processing what he'd just witnessed.

"Do you play here often?" asked Blake.

"Every week."

"Who are your opponents?"

"Anyone who wants to play."

"Thanks for agreeing to meet with me today."

"I'm delighted. Tell me your story."

"Well, this is the first time I've served as a CEO, and honestly—," Blake hesitated, then said, "I'm a bit overwhelmed."

Jack raised his hand to stop him. "No, no, we'll have plenty of time to talk about your company. Tell me *your* story."

"How far back do you want me to go?"

"How far back do you remember?"

"Okay, here we go. . . ."

Blake spent the next thirty minutes telling Jack about his childhood, his father, his father's death, his relationship with Debbie; he told him about Megan and the children and, finally, about his career at Dynastar and his transition to his new role as CEO.

"Outstanding. Now, tell me what you've discovered about your new company."

Blake took another half hour to tell Jack about his team, the lack of goals, the work ethic, the dissatisfied customers, the declining sales, and more.

"I recognize that situation," Jack offered with a faint smile.

"You do?"

"Yes, sir. I began building my career in an organization like that."

"Please tell me more!" Blake pulled out his tablet to take notes.

"As you've already discovered, what you're trying to do is extremely challenging," Jack began.

Blake nodded in agreement.

"However, the solution is closer than you think. Do you play chess?" Jack asked.

"A little, as a child. I remember some of the rules and the basic concepts." After what he had witnessed a few minutes before, he was hoping Jack didn't want to challenge him to a game.

"Do you play checkers?"

"Sure, everyone plays checkers, don't they?"

"Yes, many people play checkers." As Jack said this, he moved all the pieces off the board in front of him. He picked it up and flipped it over. On the other side were red and black squares—a checkerboard. He held up the board and turned it in the morning sun.

"One side checkers, one side chess. Have you ever noticed the two games are played on a very similar board?"

"I never thought about it, but I guess both boards do have the same number of squares."

"You are correct—sixty-four, to be exact. So what's the difference?"

"I guess just the color."

"Yes, the color is different, but that's just the beginning—the games that are played on these two, similar boards are *vastly* different."

"Your point?"

"I think I know your problem."

"Really? We just met," Blake protested mildly. Was his problem that obvious?

"Yes, I've seen it thousands of times in organizations around the world. If you want to lead a high performance organization, you've got to play chess, not checkers."

"I need to think about that a little bit," Blake said, still trying to absorb the implications of Jack's comment.

"No, you're wrong. You don't need to think about it a little—you need to think about it every day of your leadership life. If you play checkers when the name of the game is chess, you lose."

"Hold on," Blake said. "The boards are different. So how could a leader make that mistake? How could I make that mistake?"

***

If you play checkers when the name of the game is chess, you lose.

***

"Most small businesses can be successful with a checkers mindset. That's actually the game you play when an organization is in start-up mode. The leader does virtually everything in the beginning. That's checkers. Then, if you grow, you begin to add staff. Many leaders see these additional people as interchangeable pieces, nothing more than hired hands, no need for specialists. Each piece is capable of the same limited moves. That's checkers. In the beginning the game is simple. That's checkers. You react, you make decisions, the pace is frenetic—you're playing checkers. And, it works ... for a while.

"You can win in business by playing checkers until someone sneaks in one night after you've closed for the day and flips the board. The game changes, and you don't even know it."

"Why wouldn't a leader know the game has changed?"

"The change can be subtle in the beginning. When your board gets flipped, you have the same products, customers, equipment, and employees. Initially, it's easy to miss the change. Besides, when leaders are focused, we can become color-blind. The chessboard and checkerboard look identical other than their color. If you're not looking for it, you can miss the change. Leaders all over the world miss it every day."

"Tell me again why the game changes?"

"Complexity is the primary culprit. You cannot run a multimillion-dollar business like you would a lemonade stand."

"Are there signs? How can I be sure the board has really flipped?"

"The problems you encounter can be a clue."

"I've got hundreds of problems—maybe thousands," Blake chuckled.

"I'm sure you do. Many leaders discount these issues—they tend to blame them on growing pains. Sometimes they may be, but often, these problems are signals the board has been flipped, and the game has changed. If you try to play checkers in a chess world, problems are your reward."

"Can you give me an example of checkers in my business?"

"Okay. You tell me about a problem you encountered this week and how you solved it," Jack said.

"We had a major customer who sent me an email telling me they did not get their order as promised. They not only threatened to take their business elsewhere—they hinted at legal action."

"What did you do?"

"I expedited their order and flew it to them overnight."

If you try to play checkers in a chess world, problems are your reward.

Jack was waiting. "Anything else?"

"No, I think that solved the problem."

"Think again. You're playing checkers. You're just reacting—that's not the level of leadership your organization needs. You've got to elevate your leadership game." Jack's tone and directness caught Blake by surprise.

Jack continued, "Certainly, you have to do what you can to salvage a customer, but you can't stop there. Why was the order delayed to begin with? Was it an order you should have accepted in the first place? If the problem was in manufacturing, what was the root cause? Who knew about the problem before the customer contacted you? Why didn't they solve the problem? Who should have known about this problem before you got involved? What is the history on this customer? Was this order delayed because it was a custom order? Had it been delivered on time, would it have been highly profitable? If not, why do you offer this product? What did you fail to do, as the leader, because you were investing your time responding to a customer complaint? Blake, you have to think more deeply about your business."

"I don't have time to ask all those questions. And I *really* don't have time to find all the answers!" Blake startled himself with the intensity of his response.

"Checkers. You're playing checkers. When you don't have time to do your job, that's a good indication you're playing checkers. Blake, *thinking is your primary job.*"

Blake was still processing all of this when Jack continued.

"Here's another question to help reveal which game you're playing: Have you asked your employees to think deeply about the business? Have you asked them to prevent problems and solve the ones that do surface? My guess is you haven't. You, and the others on your leadership team, probably like coming to the rescue. You think *that* is your job. You like checkers. The pace and the excitement can be exhilarating. Your employees are following your lead. They are playing checkers because you are."

"That's a lot to think about." Blake was listening intently, trying to hide his emotions, but a somber look crept across his face. He thought about how much he wished he could have this conversation with his dad. Blake had suppressed his feelings ever since his father died. He missed his dad but tried to hide it and wasn't sure why this sadness resurfaced here. Maybe because the exchange with Jack reminded him of countless conversations with his dad. At the end of each one, Blake had felt both challenged and inspired.

Jack saw his reaction and offered this thought. "As we talk more, all this will become easier. There are many parallels between the type of thinking needed to excel in business and in chess. However, I'm going to simplify it for you."

"Simple would be good," Blake said thankfully.

"After leading scores of companies for many decades and playing chess my entire life, I have identified four ideas, or 'moves,' from the game that can help you, or any leader, build a high performance organization.

"Over the next few months, I'll share these moves with you. Between our meetings, you can experiment with real-world application. Along the way, we'll talk about what's working and what's not—and why.

"Let's meet again in two weeks—same time and place. Before our next meeting, look for examples of chess and checkers in your organization."

"Thank you!" Blake said.

Even though he knew how much he didn't know, chess not checkers made complete sense to him at an intuitive level. He was excited to have the chance to learn a new way to think about leadership in a complex organization. Blake was sure the board had flipped. Now he and his team just needed to learn how to play an entirely different game.

Game On!

Back at the office, Blake was anxious to share his newfound insight with the team. Already, he could think of many situations in which he and the team were clearly playing checkers.

On Monday morning, Blake arrived earlier than usual. He went to the conference room and set up both a chessboard and a game of checkers. When the team began to arrive, the comments were fun to hear.

John was the first to arrive. He looked at the table and said to Blake, "Looks like the staff failed to clean up after game night."

Brad and Angie walked in together. Brad sighed, "This is probably some lame team-building activity."

"Well, we should be good at it, because we're a pretty lame team," Angie said with a grin.

As Blake listened to each disparaging comment, he maintained a good spirit and chuckled with each jab.

After everyone was seated, Blake began. "Thanks for being here this morning. I know it's been difficult for you guys with the revolving door for CEOs over the last decade. My goal is for us to work together to make this a great organization."

"How are we going to do that?" John asked in a cynical tone.

"Well, the answer may lie in front of you." He motioned to the game boards on the conference table. "Although we know business is serious, it contains many elements of a game. I believe my problem, and our problem, is we're playing the wrong game. We have been playing checkers. Unfortunately, the game we should be playing is chess."

"Those are two really different games," Brad said in a thoughtful tone that indicated some level of interest. Blake hoped that was a sign of progress. "Tell us what you mean when you say we've been playing checkers."

"Okay, let's start with the board." Blake took the next few minutes to recap what he'd learned from Jack. He concluded by saying, "We can be so focused, we can actually become color-blind. We don't even know the game has changed."

"Are there clues?" Angie asked.

"Yes, one of the signs the game has changed is a myriad of problems—problems that reoccur; problems that should have been anticipated and avoided, problems that catch us totally by surprise and we should have seen coming, and problems that are created by lack of focus or a failure to execute. All of these are clues. When we see this happening, the methods we've used successfully in the past have to be reevaluated."

"Blake, do you think we can really learn to play chess?" Elizabeth's facial expression revealed her doubt.

"Certainly! We have a talented leadership team and people capable of outstanding work. What we are experiencing is the result of our outdated thinking. We can change our thinking. Then, we'll be able to change our approach. It's a new day and we're going to rise to the challenge."

One of the signs the game has changed is a myriad of problems.

"If not, we lose," Brad added.

"That's correct. But my promise to you and to all our employees is that we will not lose. We are going to learn a new game.

"Before we adjourn, I have an action item for each of you—I should have asked this earlier. Do any of you play chess?"

Only Elizabeth and Brad nodded.

"How well do you play?"

Elizabeth said, "I'm just an occasional player. I haven't played in years."

"Brad?"

"My rating is 2,100."

"What's that mean?" John asked.

Angie answered for him. "I think that means we have a ringer in our midst."

Blake jumped in and asked, "Brad, can you explain?"

"There's a rating system for serious players."

"Like a golf handicap?" John asked.

"Similar." Brad continued, "But unlike golf, the better you get the *higher* your rating."

"What's the top?" Charles asked.

"Grandmasters—they have ratings over 2,500."

"What do they call your level?"

Brad was hesitant. "It's the expert level."

"That's outstanding!" Blake interjected. "We have our own expert chess consultant. Now, here is your action item. Find someone, not Brad, to teach you to play chess. Pay special attention to the strategies and tactics needed to win. Take good notes on what you're learning. We're adjourned."

As everyone was leaving, Blake asked Brad to stay behind.

"What's on your mind?" Brad asked nervously.

"I realize my arrival, yet another CEO transition, has been hard," Blake paused.

"Yes, but not the hardest. Remember, I've seen this movie several times before," Brad said.

"I know. Here's my goal: I want to be the last CEO you work with."

"What's that mean?"

"I think you and I can both work here until we retire. And, I believe we can make this one of the great organizations in the world."

"What makes you think we can become great?" Brad asked.

"I know it sounds like a stretch given where we are today, but we have an amazing product, outstanding people who are grossly underutilized, a market with moderate competition, and a great CEO as my coach. We can do this!" Blake knew he was selling, but was Brad buying?

"Who's the CEO?"

"Jack Deluca."

"You know Jack Deluca?"

"Yes, he's my mentor."

"That's amazing! Based on what I've read about him, he's the real deal."

"I know," Blake agreed.

"I didn't know about Jack. Is that a secret?"

"No, it just hasn't come up."

"I think the team would be interested to know about that."

"Okay, I can tell them about Jack at our next meeting. Are you in?" Blake asked.

Brad thought for a moment and said, "If we can do what you're talking about, we can make a lot of money." He smiled, adding, "Hey, I'm the CFO—what do you expect me to say?"

"You are correct—we can make a lot of money. Let's do this!"

Brad didn't say anything. He just nodded.

"What do you think of the 'chess not checkers' idea?" Blake prodded in an attempt to further gauge Brad's buy-in.

"I think you may be on to something. We have always played checkers, reacting to this and that. Often, we're reacting to what the new CEO wants. But, it has rarely been strategic. We haven't stopped long enough to make good decisions. We're always fighting fires."

"I want to prevent the fires," Blake said.

"Me, too," Brad said. "And, if we do it right, it could be fun, too." He reached out to shake Blake's hand. "I'm in."

Start Here

As Blake drove the two hours from his home to the park, he thought about the big idea from the last meeting: chess, not checkers, is the key to leading a high performance organization. He knew there was much to do, but he had no idea where to start. He was hopeful Jack's four "moves" would make his path forward much clearer.

As he arrived at the park, the scene was almost identical—only the player across the table was different. When Blake made his presence known, Jack made one move and said, "Checkmate." Again, the opponent looked stunned, and the small crowd began to applaud.

"Thanks for coming. I'll be back next week," Jack said with a huge smile, shaking hands with a few members of the crowd as they departed.

As the last person walked away, Blake sat down and said, "That was strange."

"Really? Which part?"

"It was just like two weeks ago. Does it always end like that?"

"Like what?" Jack asked.

"Do you always win?"

"Here in the park I do, but not always."

"What's your rating?" Blake was guessing it was really high.

"2,650."

"You're a grandmaster?"

"Yes," Jack admitted.

"Why do you play here in the park?"

"It's an outstanding place to meet people. I love being outdoors. And it's close to my house. Any other questions?"

"Yes, but they're all about our last conversation," Blake said.

"Where would you like to start?"

"That's the point—I don't know where to start." Blake took the next few minutes to tell Jack about his conversations with the team. He also shared the most recent sales figures.

"Yes, the last time we met, I promised you four moves you could make to create a high performance organization."

"We need that desperately. To me, it looks like everyone in our organization is playing checkers, me included!"

"People follow successful patterns."

"We talked about that. Checkers has worked for us in the past," Blake added. "But it does appear complexity flipped the board. Can you help?"

"I believe I can. As I said, these moves, derived from winning strategies and principles from the chess world, have parallel applications in any organization."

"What's the first one?"

"In the early stages of a chess game, you work diligently to move your pieces into positions to maximize their impact. This phase is called the *development phase*. The truth is, some places on the board afford more options and flexibility. A knight positioned in the middle of the board has more power than one trapped on the side of the board.

"So, the principle is: *Develop your pieces early for maximum strategic advantage*.

You can't wait until you need a leader to start developing one.

"In a high performance organization, one way to apply this idea is to proactively develop your leadership. The earlier in their career you invest in them, the better. You can't wait until you need a leader to start developing one. I call this move **Bet on Leadership**. All high performance organizations do this."

"How did you do this in your companies?" Blake asked.

"I'll share a few thoughts, but first, a word about why this is the first of the four moves. If you don't figure this one out, you'll always struggle as an organization. You cannot be a great organization without great leadership. All the moves are critical, but this is the first among equals. Leadership growth always precedes organizational growth."

"What's my role in developing leaders?" Blake wondered out loud.

"Great question! The quest for high performance *always starts* with the leader—so does Bet on Leadership. You have got to set the pace for your team. People do what people see. If you're not learning and growing, don't expect them to, either."

Blake summarized Jack's first move like this in his notes:

Chess Not Checkers

1. Bet on Leadership

Growing leaders grow organizations

"I think I know what that looks like. Debbie has coached me on this for years."

"What will you actually do?" Jack asked. "The gap between what leaders know and do is often wide."

"The same things I've been doing. I'll get feedback from people so I can minimize my blind spots and identify gaps. Then, I'll create a multifaceted development plan. I'll read, invest time with experts, and practice the skills I'm trying to develop. I'll also continue to share what I'm learning with others. This has been a very helpful discipline for me over the years. It helps keep me sharp and accountable."

"Outstanding! Debbie has done a good job teaching you the importance of growth for a leader. Your capacity to grow determines your capacity to lead."

Blake smiled as he thought about all the times Debbie had reminded him of the same thing. "Yes, sir. I do know that. What's next?"

"To Bet on Leadership also means you'll want to invest in your team. You'll need a strong leadership team to help you execute this move and the others we'll be talking about."

Your capacity to grow determines your capacity to lead.

"How can my team help with Bet on Leadership?"

"To ensure long-term success, you must build your leadership bench. Your team can certainly help you with this. How strong is your bench today?"

"Do you mean a bench like in sports?"

"Yes. Who's next? Who are the leaders you're grooming and developing for the future? That's your leadership bench."

"I don't think we have one," Blake grinned.

"If you will identify your emerging leaders, you can begin to invest in them early. That will increase the chances they will be ready when you need them. Good chess players, and good leaders, think about the current move and the next move also—often several moves ahead. When you invest in emerging leaders, it means you're serious about creating the future rather than just hoping it works out." Jack smiled.

"That makes sense. We just haven't made it a priority." Blake jotted down a couple of notes.

"How strong is your team?" Jack asked.

"Not very strong. The individual players aren't bad, but there's not much teamwork."

"If you want your organization to thrive, you will need to strengthen your leadership team. You can't transform your organization by yourself. The challenges that are forcing you to give up checkers are the same challenges that require more leadership capacity. Your team can be your primary source of additional leadership capacity—if they're up to it. You've got to Bet on Leadership!"

"Why do you use the term 'bet'?"

"Because you can never be sure."

"Sure about what?"

"You can't be sure your investment in individual leaders will pay off. Some will rise to the challenge; some won't. Some leaders stay with the company and others leave. However, high performance organizations make the bet. They know if you can't grow your leadership capacity, you'll never reach your full potential as an organization."

"What's next for me?"

"You get to decide. What will you do to Bet on Leadership? I would suggest a conversation with your team."

"I'm on it."

"Let's meet in two weeks again. Same time, same place."

Place Your Bet

On the ride home, Blake began to think about all he'd learned in the first few months on the job. He realized leading a large and complex enterprise requires a different level of leadership. "Chess not checkers" made perfect sense conceptually. His challenge now was to figure out what it looked like in the real world. His conversation with Jack was extremely helpful. He believed his team could turn Jack's ideas into plans and tactics that would work. He was about to encounter his first real test.

On Monday morning, the team assembled at 8:00. This was beginning to feel normal, even to Elizabeth, who was not a morning person. She had already lobbied several members about moving the meeting to 8:00 p.m. The group politely declined.

As the team gathered, Blake could hear a couple of conversations around the table. It sounded to him like they were talking about chess!

"Good morning! I trust you've had a good weekend. I hear a couple of you talking about chess; we'll get to that in a moment. First, I have asked Brad to help us develop a process we can follow to create next year's plans. Brad, please give us a quick overview."

Brad reviewed the plan and schedule with the team.

"Any questions?" Blake asked.

"What's this first session about? It just says 'Visioning,'" Angie asked.

"That's the session in which we decide where we're trying to take the business. Over the years, I've found it counterproductive to do planning without a clear destination in mind."

By the body language of the group, this seemed to make sense.

"Will every department have to create a plan?" John asked.

Blake responded, "Yes, we'll create the goals and key strategies, and the individual teams will create the tactical plans. We need as many of our people involved in planning as possible. Anything else?" No one said anything. "That's fine. We'll talk a lot about the plan in the weeks ahead. Thank you, Brad."

"Now, let me tell you about my last meeting with Jack." Blake took a few minutes and talked about the first move for creating a high performance organization. He explained the concept of Bet on Leadership.

"What do we do?" Charles asked, because he had no clue where to begin. Although he had been in Human Resources for years, his expertise was in selection and compliance. The company had never charged him, or anyone else, with developing leaders. "Let's talk about that." Blake moved to a flip chart. "Tell us again what Jack suggested," Brad prodded. "He said we should lead the way and be intentional about our growth and development. That's why we Bet on Leadership—growing leaders grow organizations."

"Are you talking about us as individuals or the team?" Angie asked.

"Both," Blake said. "Jack also suggested we create a leadership bench for the future. But, let's not get ahead of ourselves. Let's start with how we might grow ourselves; then we'll talk about growing and strengthening the team. If we have time today, we'll begin conversations about the bench."

The team brainstormed for about fifteen minutes. The ideas flowed quickly.

Ideas to Help Us Grow as Individuals

- Create personal development plans
- Solicit feedback
- Accept stretch assignments
- Close critical skill gaps
- Find a coach or mentor

Next, the conversation turned to the team. This moved more slowly, in part, because the "team concept" was new to several members of the group. However, after some uncertain moments, the team had created the following list of potential developmental activities:

How Can We Help This Team Grow?

- Clarify our purpose
- Establish clear goals
- Evaluate the team on a regular basis
- Focus on team basics—better meetings, problem solving, decision making, etc.
- Build community among the team members

As the group began to review their work, Blake realized John hadn't contributed any ideas. He made a mental note and continued. "Now, let's invest a few minutes to begin thinking about how to build a leadership bench. What would we need to do to pull that off?"

Again, the team had a brief, healthy conversation about what might be required in this facet of Bet on Leadership. Still, John said nothing.

"John," Blake said, "do you have any additional ideas?"

"No. Thanks for asking."

Blake found this to be odd but decided to talk to John offline.

He ended the conversation by saying, "Thanks for sharing your thoughts today! Charles, will you please take the team's input on Bet on Leadership and come back with a recommendation for us to consider?"

"Yes," Charles cautiously agreed. "I'll need a little time."

"How much?"

"Let me bring some preliminary thoughts in a couple of weeks."

"Here's an idea," Blake responded. "Our retreat is scheduled for the end of the month; let's take a look at your recommendations then. We'll need to be sure your work syncs up with our planning process so we can budget accordingly.

"Sounds good to me," Charles agreed.

"See you all next week!" Blake said.

After the meeting, Blake went to John's office.

"John, can we talk?"

"Sure, what's on your mind?"

"How are you?"

"Why do you ask?"

"You were quiet today."

"The truth," John got up and closed his door. "I think all this stuff you're doing is crazy—the games, the team, the meetings, the planning process. And now you're suggesting we need to grow as individuals."

"Why is that strange to you?"

"I'm already grown. I don't need a development plan. All I need is for you to get out of my way so I can work."

Blake took a deep breath. He knew this was a big moment. He started slowly. "John, I respect your opinion. I know you've got a lot of years on the job."

John interrupted, "Years of experience."

"Well, John, if you're not growing, it's really just one year of experience repeated over and over again."

Blake continued, "Regarding the 'games' . . . this business is not healthy. Healthy things grow. We are not growing. So, we're going to change things to get us back on a growth path. If the 'chess not checkers' idea can help us grow the business and the people, I'm all for it."

Blake wasn't finished. "Regarding the team, I cannot lead this business alone. We need a real team— one that sets strategy, solves problems, pushes and encourages each other, and loves doing life together. Do you want to be on a team like that?"

"I just want to do my job."

"Do you want to be on the team?"

"Absolutely not. That's not what I signed up for."

"Are you sure?"

"Blake, why is this hard for you to understand? I told you, I think it's crazy."

"John, if you can't work through this, you know you can't work here any longer."

"I think you've lost your mind."

___

We need a real team—one that sets strategy, solves problems, pushes and encourages each other, and loves doing life together.

___

"I respect your decision. Thanks for your service. Charles will talk with you about your transition."

"What? Transition? Did you just fire me?" He stood up and so did Blake.

Blake calmly responded, "No, you fired yourself. Thanks for your contributions to the company over the years. We will be generous with your severance package."

What's Important?

Word spread quickly throughout the business that John was leaving. Of course, the company would be discreet and offer a statement indicating John's decision to "pursue other career options." Although that was true, Blake decided he needed to tell his team the rest of the story. So he called a special meeting for the following morning.

Just before the meeting was scheduled to begin, everyone shuffled in without saying a word. They just took their seats and looked at their new CEO, waiting for an explanation. Blake was sensitive to the mood because everyone, including Blake, had liked John.

"Good morning. I called this meeting because I know we need to talk about John's departure."

After an awkward silence, Angie said, "What happened? John had worked here for years."

"I know. I hated that he decided to leave."

"Did he really, or did you fire him?" Brad asked.

"No, I didn't fire him. I outlined what I expected from a member of my senior team, and he said he didn't want to be part of it. I respect that."

"What did you tell him? I guess we should all know. Maybe some of us will make a similar decision," Charles said.

"I told him three things were required: First, the willingness and ability to grow with the business. We cannot let it outgrow us. Next, a desire to help transform this organization so it can reach its full potential. And, finally, I told John he had to want to be on this team. I need this team to become a high performance leadership team, and the first step on that journey is a desire to make it so.

I really believe we have greatness in our future— *if* we work together.

"Obviously, one or more of these expectations were outside his comfort zone, and he decided to leave. Any questions?" Blake waited a moment and then continued. "I hope each of you can make a commitment to those things. I really believe we have greatness in our future—*if* we work together. I can't do this alone, and neither can you. We really do need each other. If you have concern over any of these expectations, let's talk."

If there had been any doubt before, it was now clear—it was a new day.

■ ■ ■

The time had come for Blake's next visit with Jack. He wanted to tell him about John's departure. He wasn't sure how Jack would respond, but at least he could get some coaching. Blake was also anxious to learn his next move on their journey to high performance.

The bright, clear morning and warmth of the season were bringing the park to life. From the looks of the situation, the nice weather had increased the size of the gallery at Jack's table as well.

When Jack saw Blake in the crowd, he announced to the crowd, "It looks like my next appointment has arrived. I'll concede this game."

His opponent, a young woman, seemed delighted. She asked Jack, "Does that mean I can tell people I won today?"

"Yes, please do," Jack said with a big smile.

After Jack shook hands with several members of the gallery, he turned to Blake. "Good to see you again." This morning, rather than shake Blake's hand as he had done on previous visits, Jack gave him a hug.

Blake, a bit surprised, said, "Thanks, Jack."

"Well, I thought you could use a hug today."

"Why did you think that?"

Jack shrugged. "I don't know. You've just got that look about you today." Apparently, John's departure was affecting Blake's demeanor.

"Well, I guess I'm still wondering if I did the right thing."

"About what?"

"John is gone."

"Did he quit?"

"Sort of." Blake paused. "It was a combination of resignation and termination." He proceeded to tell Jack the entire story.

"Congratulations, Blake."

"For what?"

"For your willingness to make the hard call. My confidence in your future success just rose significantly."

"Really? All I did was make a change in leadership."

"That single step is one many leaders are unable to take."

"They can't?"

"They cannot muster the courage to do the right thing."

"I hope it was the right thing," Blake said.

"Based on what you told me, it was the right thing for the team, for the business, and for John."

"I understand the 'for the team' and 'for the business' part, but say a little more about why letting John go was good for him."

"I believe every human has within them the potential to be successful. The release of this potential is contingent on several factors, including their desire, their effort, the right work, and the right place to apply their talents. If a person can't thrive in your environment and you release him or her to find another place better suited for them, you've given them a gift. To allow someone to stay in the wrong job is an epic leadership failure. John admitted he was in the wrong job. You helped him escape."

"Thanks for that. It seemed like the right thing to do in the moment. Your comments are reassuring. Now, I'm ready for what's next."

To allow someone to stay in the wrong job is an epic leadership failure.

"Today, we need to talk about the second move you need to make if you want to embrace a chess not checkers game plan. But before we go there, give me an update on your progress with Bet on Leadership. We don't want to miss that one. Everything rises and falls on leadership, you know."

"Yes, you said it was foundational, and we're working on it. I'm learning and trying to apply what we're discussing. I think that counts as setting the pace. Charles is creating a preliminary plan for us to review regarding how we can systematically develop future leaders. And, as strange as it may sound, I believe John's departure will strengthen my leadership team."

"I understand completely," Jack said. "Strength through subtraction—when you have the wrong person at the table, it siphons energy from the rest of the team. I see it all the time. Now, you must capitalize on John's departure by finding an outstanding replacement."

"Yes, the team and I are talking about how to move forward with the search."

Jack asked, "Are you ready to move?"

"Yes. Thanks for helping me work through the issue with John. I feel better by just talking about it," Blake said.

Jack nodded, "Today, we are going to talk about one of the most often missed opportunities in businesses all over the world. I have personally witnessed this next move single-handedly derail organizations and revolutionize others. It, too, is built on a simple idea from the game of chess: *A unified assault is always preferred over a fragmented one.*

"Here's how this principle plays out in the world of chess. Imagine you want to attack one of your opponent's pieces. To do so effectively requires focusing multiple resources on that single piece. To attack with one is futile—your piece will be lost. As a result, the best players don't usually attack on too many fronts simultaneously. That approach spreads needed resources too thin and is not a winning strategy. To randomly attack—a piece to the left and one to the right—applies little, if any pressure, on your opponent. You've got to make your pieces work together to maximize your assault."

A unified assault is always preferred over a fragmented one.

"Got it. So the move is . . . ?" Blake waited.

"**Act as One**," Jack said. "Blake, what's important in your business?"

Without hesitation, Blake said, "Our purpose, mission, and values to start with; then, I guess key goals would be important, too."

"Is all of that crystal clear in your mind?"

"No, not really—not yet," Blake admitted.

"Then it cannot be clear for your organization. Act as One is about getting *everyone* in your organization pulling on the rope in the same direction. That's a prerequisite to unleash the full potential of your business. Getting everyone aligned can have a phenomenal impact on your performance. I've seen it countless times."

Blake grabbed his tablet and wrote:

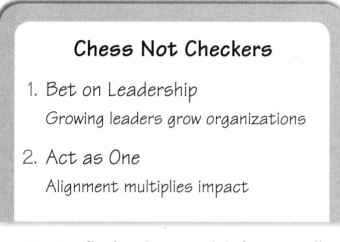

Chess Not Checkers

1. Bet on Leadership

   Growing leaders grow organizations

2. Act as One

   Alignment multiplies impact

"Yes, I realize how important it is for us to pull on the rope in the same direction. That's why I was so amazed when I realized the organization had no goals when I arrived."

"It is hard to imagine leaders who ask people to give their best without helping them know what success looks like," Jack said.

"Or, why it matters," Blake added.

"So, in terms of next steps, I have three recommendations: One, decide what's important to you. Two, get agreement from your leadership team. And, finally, begin an orchestrated effort to cascade and reinforce these messages throughout your organization."

"Sounds fairly straightforward," Blake said.

"Yes, but don't miss the power of each step: Decide, agree, and communicate. Most leaders fumble the ball somewhere in the process."

"How does that happen?" Blake asked.

"Often the leader is clear on what matters most, and his or her key leaders know, too—and yet everyone else remains in the dark. The information never reaches the front lines in the organization. This is a colossal leadership mistake. You can't harness the power of everyone unless everyone is in the know. You will never really Act as One unless you master cascading communications!"

"Thanks for the challenge and the steps. I'm excited to say we've already begun!"

"Great! What are you doing?"

You will never really Act as One unless you master cascading communications!

"We've initiated a planning process with the leadership team. We're going to identify what we need to align around. We're going to work on at least four things: a long-term vision, core values, goals, and key strategies. Then, we'll involve the entire team to build tactical plans. Anything else I need to know about Act as One?"

"Yeah! There's a lot you need to know." Jack laughed out loud. "But you'll learn."

"You're right. That was a bad question. Let me rephrase it. Is there anything else you want to tell me *today* about Act as One?"

"I'm glad you asked," Jack smiled. "Just one last thing—don't assume alignment is something you can fix and walk away; it will be an ongoing challenge. Think of your organization as a car driving at high speeds down a bumpy, dirt road. The car will constantly be knocked out of alignment. Part of your never-ending role is to keep the organization aligned on what matters most. When your organization gets out of alignment, you lose energy, focus, momentum, and results."

"Thanks for the reminder. I assumed we would work on this forever."

"You are correct."

"Before I go, I have one more question. Can you say a little bit about high performance? That's language you use a lot. It may be obvious, and I certainly have my own definition, but what do you mean when you use the term?"

"High performance should be the goal of every organization. When superior results and competitive advantage are achieved and maintained over an extended period of time, that's high performance. A good month or a good quarter should be celebrated, but it should not be confused with high performance. The perennial winner in any field of endeavor—that's my definition of high performance."

"Fantastic! That's what I thought you meant."

"Anything else we need to talk about today?" Jack asked.

Blake thought for a second and said, "One more thing. I asked my team to learn to play chess."

"Nice move," Jack said with a slight smile.

"Thanks. Can you help me learn the game?"

When your organization gets out of alignment, you lose energy, focus, momentum, and results.

"I'm not sure; that's beyond the scope of my normal consulting agreement," Jack said.

Blake wasn't sure if Jack was serious or not. "I will pay it forward," he said.

"Okay, then, I'll do it. Teaching you the game will require some extra time, so let's schedule separate meetings for that. I don't want us to lose traction on what you're trying to do with your organization. I'll also send you a good book to explain some of the basics."

"Thank you. See you in two weeks!"

■ ■ ■

As he drove toward his office, Blake began to think of ways to help his leaders, and the entire business, understand what it means to Act as One. He also wanted to find ways to help people understand the importance of shared vision and values.

When Blake arrived at the office, he stopped by to visit with Brad.

Brad was an interesting guy. A finance person by training and occupation, he was not your typical accountant. He was different from the rest of Blake's team in many ways. For starters, he had not been affected by the new dress code—he had always been on the forefront of style. He usually looked like he had just come from the cover of a very trendy magazine. Blake was also reminded of Brad's atypical work style as he approached his "space." Brad didn't have a traditional office.

"Knock, knock," Blake said as he approached Brad's imaginary door. This work setting fit Brad's offbeat personality perfectly. It included a sofa, coffee table and a large whiteboard on wheels but no walls or door.

"Who's there?" Brad said in a playful tone Blake had never heard from Brad.

"I wish I knew a good 'knock-knock' joke, but I don't," Blake apologized.

"That's okay, I've heard them all. What can I do for you this afternoon?"

"Why don't you have an office?"

"Excuse me? Is that why you came by?" Brad asked.

"No, no. I have something else to ask you, but I realized we never talked about why you don't have an office. You know you can if you want one."

"Thanks for the offer. I gave up my office years ago."

"Why?"

"It's important to me for people to know I'm accessible. It's the ultimate open-door policy—since I don't have a door," Brad explained.

"Interesting." Blake sat there thinking.

"You said you had a question."

"Yes, but I think this conversation is related. You don't have an office, because you are trying to communicate something important—your accessibility. I came to tell you what Jack and I talked about today— Act as One. It's about all of us being aligned on what matters most. He challenged me to figure out what's important around here and then decide how to be sure everyone knows."

"How do we do that?" Brad asked.

"I think the ball is in our court. We have to let people know where we are headed and how we'll behave along the way."

"How can I help?"

"Come to the first planning meeting ready to create the future."

■ ■ ■

Blake was excited about the senior team's first planning meeting. From his perspective, the timing was perfect.

"Good morning! Thanks for carving out a day to begin creating the future!" Blake's energy reflected the importance he placed on this meeting and the process he and the team were beginning today. "I have always believed planning is one of a leader's most important responsibilities."

"Are you serious? We've never given much attention to it before. In the years we've done a plan, we just created something that went in a file. We never looked at it again," Charles said in a moment of transparency.

Elizabeth added in a joking tone, "How's that working out for us?"

Several members of the team chuckled.

"I am serious about the importance of planning, Charles. Thanks for asking the question.

"Do you know what leaders do?" Blake said, turning his eyes from Charles to the team.

"Lead?" Elizabeth said.

"Yes. To what end?"

"To accomplish goals," Brad said.

"You're getting closer," Blake said. "Leaders are the architects of the future." He paused to let that idea sink in. Then he continued. "Our plan is the blueprint for the future we're going to create. And, the plan helps us get everyone in the organization aligned."

"Exactly what do you mean by 'aligned'?" Charles asked.

Leaders are the architects of the future.

Blake took the next few minutes to explain Act as One. He focused on the idea of everyone pulling on the rope in the same direction. "To do that well, the entire organization must be on the same page. The plan enables us to move closer to being fully aligned."

"One more thing about planning," Blake continued. "As we've learned in recent weeks, chess is a game of choices, and business is, too. We win or lose based on our choices and how well we execute against those choices. Planning is where we make those fundamental choices."

"So what are we going to do today?" Brad asked.

"I know this is ambitious," Blake began, "but I'd like us to decide what's most important around here."

Blake went to the flip chart and wrote three questions:

1. Why are we here?

2. What does success look like in 10 years?

3. What beliefs will shape how we do our work?

"These are the questions we need to answer today if we can. The first, 'Why are we here?' will help us address the issue of purpose. The next will help us define our mission, and the third will help us articulate our core values.

"Let's start with an activity," Blake said. "On the table in front of you, you'll find a 3 × 5 card. Take one of those and answer the first question: Why are we here?"

Everyone worked quickly, then handed Blake their cards. After he collected all the cards, he read each one out loud. Each idea was thoughtful, but each was different. After Blake finished reading, the group just sat there.

Elizabeth was the first to comment. "No wonder we don't Act as One—we don't even agree on why we're here!"

"The good news is we can fix that," Charles said.

"So why are we here?" Blake asked.

The next hour was very insightful for Blake and the entire team. The conversation became animated at several points, which Blake interpreted as a good thing. After much debate, Blake walked to the flip chart and said, "Here's what I'm hearing. . . ."

Our Purpose

Grow People and Grow the Business

The team seemed to like it.

"We can Act as One around that," Brad said. "Although I still wish it said, 'Profitably' at the end."

That sparked a short debate, and the team agreed they would be sure people understood the profit imperative.

"It's clean and simple," Angie said. "I can talk about it. More important, I think we can do it. What's next?"

The team then launched into a conversation about long-term success. They were attempting to answer the question of their mission.

"It's really hard to establish *one* goal," Brad insisted.

"It is, but if we can set the right one, it could drastically increase our focus. We will still have a scorecard containing multiple metrics. We just need to decide what the primary goal is that will drive the right behaviors throughout the organization." The team invested a couple of hours discussing dozens of ideas. At the end of the debate, Blake wrote on the flipchart:

Our Mission

#1 Market Share in a Decade

"Where are we now in terms of market share?" Elizabeth asked.

"I'm guessing we're seventh or eighth," Blake said.

"We'll need a lot more sales to be number one," Charles said.

"How much more?" Blake asked.

"We'll probably need another $3 to $4 million a year, depending on what our competitors do."

"That's exciting!" Angie said.

"We are going to have to replace John," Brad reminded the group. "And we should probably do that soon."

"We're also going to need to increase our production capacity."

"Is it doable?" Brad asked.

"I think so," Elizabeth said.

Blake asked the group, "Are we good?"

Everyone looked pleased. "Let's go forward with this. We have time to sleep on it before we share it with others, but it feels right to me," Blake said as he scanned the faces of the men and women at the table. "Brad, please put together a communications plan. Let's review your recommendations at our retreat."

"Yes, sir," Brad said.

Finally, the group turned its attention to the question of core values. Blake opened the conversation, saying, "I want to tell you now, this is going to be a consultative decision. I have some strong feelings about this topic, but I need your best thinking— please don't hold back."

"Exactly what does 'consultative decision' mean?" Brad asked.

"It means, Blake is going to decide," Angie laughed.

"You are correct," Blake said in a light-hearted tone. "I am going to decide with your input. I really want to hear your thoughts. Who wants to start the conversation?"

Angie asked, "And exactly what are core values?"

Elizabeth fielded this one. "They're the beliefs that drive your behavior."

"Thanks, Elizabeth. So what are ours?" Blake asked.

This simple question started the most animated conversation yet. After a couple of hours, Blake said, "Let's take a break. Everyone come back in thirty minutes with your recommended top five."

The group came back refreshed. Blake began this final session of the day by asking everyone to read his or her list. He wrote all the possibilities on the flip-chart. The overlap was affirming; on three out of five, there was no debate.

When Blake stopped writing, Angie looked at him and asked, "Which of these can you support?"

"All of mine are on the board," he said, not yet wanting to show his hand.

"We have total agreement on three," Charles said. "None of the others are bad. Blake, you make the call."

Blake looked around the room, "Anybody else have comments you would like to share at this point?"

Blake wasn't sure if the silence was fatigue, resignation, or general agreement. He decided to push forward. "Okay. Here are the five."

Our Core Values

Passion	All in or not at all
Learning	The origin of our long-term success
Participation	Everyone participates—no spectators
Creativity	The source of our competitive advantage
Collaboration	Together, we honor everyone's strengths

"Wow!" Elizabeth said. "Do you guys realize what we did today? For the first time ever, we actually began to Act as One."

Blake felt really good about the work of the team. "Okay, let's continue to think about what we did today. We'll put it on the agenda for our next meeting. That will be the last call for any questions or concerns before we move forward.

"Thank you for your work today. We're going to look back and see this meeting, and our decisions here, as a defining moment for our team, our organization, and us as leaders. We're positioning ourselves for an amazing future. Thank you!"

Who Cares?

For the first time in his short career as a CEO, Blake felt like the team was finally on track. If he was honest with himself, he was embarrassed it had taken him several months to get this far. Thank goodness Debbie had introduced him to Jack. The "chess not checkers" moves Jack was suggesting were easy to understand and communicate. He knew what Jack was teaching him would take time to fully implement. But at least for now, he felt the team was on the right path.

It was time for Blake to meet with Jack again. The team had already begun to implement ideas around Bet on Leadership and Act as One—they were making progress! Blake was energized as he thought about his upcoming meeting.

Once again, the park was relatively empty—except around Jack's table. Again on this morning, Blake found Jack playing a game with a small crowd watching. After Jack spotted Blake, it took several moves before he made his final move and announced, "Checkmate." And, as usual, the bystanders went wild—this was not a typical chess crowd.

As the crowd departed, Blake sat down across from Jack. "How are you?"

"Fantastic, and you?" Jack asked.

"Really good. I think we're finally starting to get it. And, I've been reading the book you gave me about chess. It really is a challenging game."

"What are you learning?"

"A lot! When I played as a child, I didn't know any of the strategies. All I really knew was what each piece could do and a few of the rules."

"Learning to play the game was a good idea, Blake. It will provide a good foundation we can build on and give you additional perspective as we look at the other moves your organization needs to make. Today, let's start with what has happened since our last meeting," Jack suggested.

Blake took a few minutes to share the progress on Act as One and the work of the team.

"What's next?"

"In our first meeting, we talked about the differences between chess and checkers."

"Yes, I remember," Blake said.

"One of those key differences deserves a little more attention."

"What's that?"

"In checkers, the pieces are basically interchangeable; each is allowed to move only on the diagonal squares. In chess, there are different types of pieces, each with its own unique moves. To be successful in chess, you want to understand and capitalize on these differing and unique capabilities. Here's the principle: *The more you can leverage the unique capabilities of each piece, the greater your chances of victory.*

"Here's an example from the game. Did you know each chess piece is assigned a point value?"

"No, I didn't," Blake said.

"Yes, a queen is worth nine points, a rook is five and a bishop is three, and so forth. These values establish relative strength and can help you decide when an exchange is worth making. Here's what you may find interesting as you think about leveraging unique capabilities: Although the bishop is only worth three points, two bishops working in tandem are worth *seven*. When used strategically, they create greater value.

The more you can leverage the unique capabilities of each piece, the greater your chances of victory.

"This is the way you need to look at your people. When you deploy them thoughtfully, you create greater value."

"Just like the bishops deployed wisely create additional value," Blake said.

"Exactly," Jack said. "When you work diligently to discover and leverage people's unique contributions, you unleash latent value and contribution."

"So what's the move?"

"High performance organizations work to **Win the Heart**," Jack said.

"You're going to have to connect the idea of leveraging unique skills with Win the Heart," Blake said.

"Gladly. When people are given the opportunity to do what they do best, you engage much more than their hands. When you allow people to contribute their unique gifts and ask them to work from a place of personal strength, you do much more than get work done—you honor them and their contribution.

"Some leaders are satisfied if people show up on time and do what they are told. That's an extremely low bar. What I'm advocating, and what you want, are men and women who are *fully* engaged. When this happens, you unleash tremendous untapped potential in every one of them."

"I'm afraid we're not too good at that," Blake admitted.

"Most organizations aren't, but the great ones are: they create a place in which people willingly invest themselves fully in the work of the organization. When you create that type of environment, people respond at a deep, heartfelt level. You can literally win their hearts and discover a wellspring of energy and contribution in the process."

"Is leveraging unique contribution all that's required to Win the Heart?"

"No, I wish it were that easy. That's just the starting point."

"What else can we do?"

"Like everything we have discussed, there is no quick fix. To Win the Heart is a process. To further complicate matters, when you are trying to win someone's heart, one size doesn't fit all. By that, I mean activities that will raise one person's engagement may not work with someone else."

"I've seen that before. While leading my team at Dynastar, I realized I had to treat people differently."

"That's a sign of leadership maturity. If you have a manager's mentality, you tend to treat people all the same. Leaders understand if you want to bring out the best in each person, you must treat them differently." Jack continued. "However, I do have a few ideas that seem to have broad application."

"I would love to know what those are."

"Okay, here's one that may stretch your thinking: foster dreams."

"I have two questions," Blake said. "First, what does that mean?"

"Help people find and fulfill their dreams. Your second question?"

"What's that got to do with chess?"

"Nothing." Jack smiled. "But it's still true. If you help people accomplish their dreams, you'll take another step toward winning their heart."

"I don't think I would have ever come up with that one on my own. I have to confess, it does seem strange."

"Call it what you will; if you help an employee go back to college, or buy a house, or learn to speak English, or become a lawyer, or buy a new car, or whatever *they* dream of doing, everyone wins."

"And we can win their heart," Blake said. He thought for a moment and added, "It's probably not something our competitors are trying to do, either."

"You are correct. Most employers are trying to *extract* value from their people. If you foster dreams, you'll be *adding* value to their lives. It's a totally different orientation."

"Our purpose does say we want to help people grow. This sounds like one more way to accomplish that objective. Thanks. What else do I need to know?"

"Have you considered giving people real responsibility?"

"I think we do that now. Exactly what are you talking about?"

"Most people want to do more, be more, and contribute more. Giving them real responsibility is one way to fulfill that desire. Giving people real responsibility also communicates that you trust them."

"I'm guessing it also accelerates their growth when you ask them to do something challenging."

Most employers are trying to *extract* value from their people. If you foster dreams, you'll be *adding* value to their lives.

"Yes, but let me give you a point of clarification. I'm not talking about just assigning tasks. Certainly you will continue to do that as needed, but I'm talking about assigning outcomes. When people know the outcome you want or need and you don't tell them *how* to get it done, their responsibility meter comes alive.

"All of these actions together create a winning combination. If you do these things well, you'll not only Win the Hearts of your employees—you can also create competitive advantage. You'll be able to recruit and retain top talent."

Jack continued, "Here's the best part. You're already paying for their hands—and with every pair of hands you hire, you get a free brain. The key to unlock that brain lies in the heart. When you get the head, the heart, and the hands, you've tapped a deep well of passion, creativity, and performance."

"Anything else?"

"One more thing—and it's probably the bottom line. You must show them you care."

"Who?"

"Anyone whose heart you want to win. Every person on your team, from the most junior to the most senior, wants to know 'Do you care about me?' When they know the answer to that question is yes, they tend to reciprocate—caring begets caring."

Blake attempted to summarize Jack's counsel as he added to his notes:

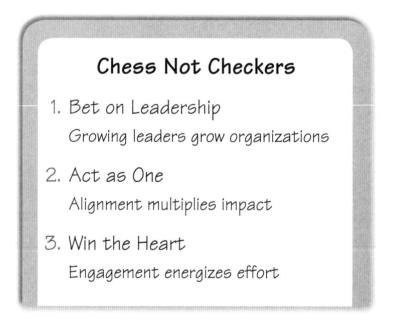

Chess Not Checkers

1. Bet on Leadership
   Growing leaders grow organizations

2. Act as One
   Alignment multiplies impact

3. Win the Heart
   Engagement energizes effort

As he finished writing, he looked up and Jack was standing. He extended his hand to Blake. "Thanks for coming today. Let's meet again in two weeks—and next time, we're actually going to play chess."

Blake frowned and said, "That should be a short meeting."

"See you in two weeks!"

■ ■ ■

At the office, Blake was preoccupied with two things: discovering how to win people's hearts and finding John's replacement. He knew the heart issue was important, but finding someone to fill John's role seemed urgent.

Blake sat at his desk staring out the window, as Suzy came to the door. "Blake . . . Blake . . . Blake," she said, raising her voice slightly each time.

"Yes, I'm sorry, I was. . . ."

"Thinking again?" She smiled.

"Yes, I was thinking."

"About what?"

"I've been challenged recently about helping our staff members leverage their strengths. How do you determine what someone does well, what they were born to do?" He said, still thinking, not really intending Suzy to answer.

"You could ask them."

"What?"

"You could ask them what they love to do. If you ask people about their passions and gifts, I'm guessing most folks will tell you."

"How about you?" Blake asked Suzy.

"How about me, what?"

"When are you at your best?"

"I love connecting people. I'm a networker."

"Really? I didn't know that about you."

"See what you can learn about people when you ask!"

"Did you have a question?"

"I came in to tell you the candidate for John's job called and decided not to come today."

"He wants to reschedule the appointment?"

"Not exactly. He said he changed his mind and doesn't want to interview for the job."

Blake's shoulders slumped. "He was our lead candidate. Thanks for letting me know."

"If you want me to help out with John's work until you find his replacement, let me know."

"That's kind of you. Do you know anything about marketing?"

"Well, I told you, I'm a connector." Suzy paused. "And, I have a master's in marketing from Northwestern."

"You do?"

"Yes, sir. Burned out at a big agency—I came here to recover and never left."

Blake sat looking at her in disbelief. Before he could decide what to say next, Suzy said, "It's amazing what you can learn about people if you ask them." She turned and left with a big smile on her face.

Could Suzy really serve as the head of Marketing?
That would be crazy, he thought. However, he didn't
have time to do the work himself. He decided he
would talk to some of his team about Suzy pinch-
hitting while he interviewed other candidates. It wouldn't
be the craziest thing he had ever done—the thought
of playing chess with Jack came immediately to mind.

■ ■ ■

At the next leadership team meeting, Blake shared
what he had learned from Jack about the third move:
Win the Heart. He reminded his team that just like
chess pieces, each person on their team had unique
talents, gifts, and capabilities. They were not interchangeable pieces.

Blake concluded this conversation by asking
everyone to meet with each member of his or her
respective teams before the next meeting. "Ask them
to share their strengths, passions, and interests. Take
good notes. We'll review all of it when we get back
together. I've recently been reminded, you can learn a
lot about someone by asking."

Blake ended their time together by surfacing the
issue of Suzy filling in while they looked for John's
replacement.

"I think we should give her a chance. Who knows?
She may be great," Elizabeth said.

"Well," Charles said, "this entire conversation highlights the need to develop future leaders. It's too bad we don't have anyone on John's team who can step up."

"You're right, but we don't," Angie said in a matter-of-fact tone.

"What do we have to lose?" Brad asked.

"Not much," Charles said.

"Okay, I've heard enough—we will ask Suzy to join this team as Interim Director of Marketing," Blake said.

It's Your Move

The business continued to improve—or so it seemed. The team was now interacting between meetings. Suzy was doing much better than anyone expected. She was open to feedback, and she asked outstanding questions. Blake hired a temporary assistant, Alex, so Suzy could focus on her new role. Then, on the day before Blake's next meeting with Jack, things took a turn—a big turn—for the worse.

Blake had arrived early to slay the email dragon before it grew in strength. He had made several positive changes over the previous weeks, and the number of messages was steadily decreasing. His team now owned many of the issues once funneled directly to him. From his perspective, this was a very good sign. However, quite a few messages still made their way to him. This morning, he found one that captured his full attention. The subject line read, "We're Done!"

As Blake quickly read the message, his heart rate increased. He scrolled back to the top to confirm the sender—unfortunately, it was their biggest client. They were leaving. They were not satisfied with the service, the product, or the attitude of Blake's company.

He wanted to scream. The lagging sales of the previous few months would now become a clear declining trend line. His mind raced ... maybe he could salvage the customer. He wanted to call. However, the email ended with this: "Don't waste your breath calling. I won't take your call. We're done!"

Blake called an unscheduled leadership team meeting. Everyone arrived, not knowing what was up.

"We have an issue. I received an email this morning from Sam Everett. For those of you who don't know, he is our biggest customer. Actually, he *was* our biggest customer."

"Did he die?" Angie asked.

"No," Blake said, trying to stay calm. "He has taken his business elsewhere."

"That's not good—the truth is, that's terrible," Brad said, with a grimace.

"Yes, that's bad. Our sales trend now is definitely headed south."

"What happened?" Charles asked.

"He's fed up with our 'poor products and service.' He also says we've not been responsive to his concerns. I will send you all the email, and you can read it yourself. Elizabeth, I want you to dig into this. Help us find specifics. We may not get answers from Sam. He said he wouldn't talk to us, but learn what you can.

"People, we cannot ever let this happen again. If we're going to accomplish the things we've been talking about, we need new customers *and* we need to keep the ones we've already won. I don't have anything else for you right now.

"Elizabeth, be prepared to give us a full report at our next meeting. If there's anything we can do before then, let us know. Adjourned." Blake walked out leaving everyone sitting around the conference room table.

■ ■ ■

The next morning, Blake drove faster than usual to his meeting with Jack. He was anxious to tell him about Sam's defection and glean whatever wisdom he could. In the park, it was the same scene as before. Blake saw a small crowd gathered around Jack's table and what he assumed was another novice learning the power of a grandmaster.

As he made his way through the crowd, he was taken aback to see Brad sitting across the table from Jack. Blake and the others watched in silence. Although still a novice, Blake had a sense this game was different than the ones he had watched Jack play before. First, there were far fewer pieces left on the board. And, Jack's facial expression and body language made it appear he was concentrating more deeply. After a few moments, Jack made his move, but it was not checkmate as Blake might have anticipated. Jack said, "Check."

Brad quickly made his move.

Jack smiled and said, "Good effort." He then moved a single pawn and said, "Checkmate."

Everyone began to clap, including Blake. It appeared as though Brad offered a little more challenge than Jack's usual opponents.

"Thanks, everyone. See you next week."

As Brad stood to leave, Blake smiled and said, "Sit back down. You have some explaining to do."

"It's really very simple. You challenged us to find someone to teach us to play chess. Since I already knew how to play, I wanted to find someone to help me play better. I sent Jack an email asking him for a game."

Brad stood a second time to leave, "I do need to get back to the office. Thanks, Jack. I enjoyed our game. Hopefully, we can play again."

"I hope we can. You know where my office is." Jack motioned to the table in front of them.

After Brad left, Blake said. "Thanks for coaching us. More and more, I'm understanding this 'chess not checkers' mindset has far-reaching implications."

"Yes, it does. What's on your agenda for today?"

"A lot. But before we jump in, I noticed something today at the end of your game with Brad."

"What was that?"

"You checkmated him with a pawn. I didn't know you could do that."

"Yes, you can. Why does that surprise you?"

"The pawn has the least amount of power, mobility, and even the lowest point value of all the pieces."

"Correct, but it's a great metaphor for what you and I have been talking about. The pawn is always a crucial element in victory. Sometimes, as you saw today, it's even the pawn that delivers the final blow. In a 'chess not checkers' approach to leadership, the moves you're learning are intended to marshal *all* your resources to help you accomplish your objectives. Front-line workers—your so-called pawns—are critical to your success; even though you might think their power is limited, you can't win without them."

"Thanks for that reminder. I've just never seen a pawn take down a king," Blake said.

"Oh, I think you have."

"When?"

"You're the fifth CEO in ten years at your company?"

"Correct."

"Who took down those previous CEOs? Was it the competition? Was there a coup d'état? I'm guessing poor execution at the front lines brought down those leaders. If the front-line people aren't performing and the leader can't correct the situation, the leader will fall. Never underestimate the power of those on the front lines doing the work."

Blake sat in silence.

"Are you okay?"

"I'm just thinking. One of the things I wanted to discuss today was ... we lost our biggest client. You've just shed new light on why they decided to leave us."

"What happened?" Jack asked.

Blake proceeded to tell Jack everything about Sam and the lost account.

Never underestimate the power of those on the front lines doing the work.

"This is perfect," Jack said.

"Perfect?" Blake was indignant. "What's perfect about it?"

"It's the perfect setup for the fourth move." Jack continued, "How good are you at the execution in your business?"

"Exactly what are you referring to?"

"In football, you'd call it blocking and tackling. In the overnight package delivery business, you'd look at on-time rates to answer my question. In restaurants, you might look at operational or customer satisfaction metrics. My question is simply this: how good are you at delivering what your customers pay you to do?"

"Sadly, we're not great," Blake said.

"You can change!" Jack offered with urgency in his voice. "If you don't, you'll never win consistently."

"So, what's the final move? I hope it can help us here."

"It's what we've just been talking about. **Excel at Execution**—that's the fourth move. In the end, execution is what separates the great organizations from all the rest," Jack said emphatically.

"Okay. How does that relate to chess?"

"It's derived from a principle simple to articulate and challenging enough to warrant a lifetime of pursuit: *If you consistently make the right moves at the right time, you win.*"

Jack continued, "In chess, it's always best to be intentional and strategic—no wasted moves. However, the right move is sometimes determined by your strategy and sometimes by circumstances outside your control. If you see your opponent shifting resources toward a weak area in your line, you don't wait to see if he or she is bluffing—you move! To move too late is equivalent to not moving at all. The right move involves intentionally deploying the right resources at the right time for maximum effect.

"In business, the implications are infinite. This principle explains why it's much better to build quality into the process versus inspecting to remove defects. It explains why preventive maintenance is preferred to downtime due to equipment failure. It explains why training people before they assume a role is preferred to the cleanup often required after they've tried and failed.

"Besides, any plan is only as good as your execution. If you don't execute, you will not win in business or in chess.

"You must execute—great organizations Excel at Execution."

Blake made a quick note:

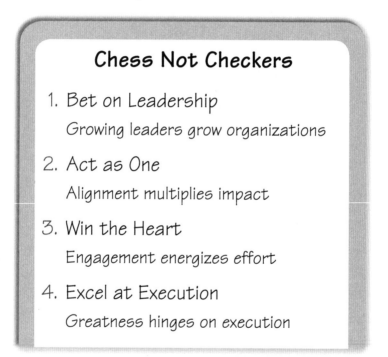

Chess Not Checkers

1. Bet on Leadership

    Growing leaders grow organizations

2. Act as One

    Alignment multiplies impact

3. Win the Heart

    Engagement energizes effort

4. Excel at Execution

    Greatness hinges on execution

Jack asked, "How much time do you devote to execution?"

"Are you kidding me? That's all we talk about," Blake protested.

"Talk is cheap," Jack offered in a serious tone. "Are you executing at a higher level today than you did thirty days ago?"

"I'm not sure ... uh ... I don't think so."

"First, you should *know* the answer to that question."

Blake made a quick note to find the answer when he got back to the office.

"To help your team improve execution, measure what matters most. Have you set any goals for the business?"

"We've talked about a long-term mission."

"Outstanding! What about short-term goals?"

"We have not worked on those yet."

"I suggest you do that soon. And once you've set those goals, be sure to share the score with the entire team. People love to keep score. You may also need to teach the basics of business to your team members so the score makes more sense."

"Do you really think everyone wants to know the score?"

"Without a doubt! If there is no measurement, work quickly becomes drudgery. Meaningful measurement will bring energy, focus, and improvement to any area of your business."

"We need to work on this. My leadership team hasn't had a scorecard in the past. Therefore, I'm guessing they aren't sharing the score with their people."

"It sounds like you have a lot of people just going through the motions."

That hurt, but Blake had no reasonable defense—Jack was probably right. "Anything else?" he said weakly.

To help your team improve execution, measure what matters most.

"To improve execution, be sure your business is built on systems, not on personality."

"You're going to have to say a little more about that one," Blake requested.

"Systems are replicable—personality is not. You don't want something to be done with excellence only because a certain person is doing it. As an example, you don't want a selection process that works because one person makes good people decisions—that's checkers. What if that person leaves or dies? You want to build a *system* capable of making good people selections—that's chess."

"What else can we do?"

"I'll give you a couple more," Jack said, as if he had a dozen ideas on the tip of his tongue. "This one is related to sharing the score: communicate performance visually. Charts, graphs, and other creative means of communication will help people focus on the fundamentals."

"You mentioned 'creative means' of communicating. Can you give me an example?"

"Is waste an issue for you guys?"

"Sure. It's true for us and all of our competitors."

"Have you ever considered a display?"

"A display of what?"

"A display of waste."

"Really?"

"It's just an idea, but you need to do whatever it takes to communicate with your people. Sometimes, seeing is believing."

Blake added this to his list of ideas even though it seemed odd to him in the moment—a display of waste?

"One last idea: narrow your focus. You said the customer you lost had several issues."

"Yes."

"You can't attack all the problems at one time. If you want to significantly improve execution in any arena, you will need to focus."

"How do I know where we should focus?"

"Just like in chess, you will need to think deeply, choose wisely, and act decisively; every move counts. Excel at Execution—that's how you ultimately win the game. It's not the team with the most elaborate game plan; it's the team that can successfully run the plays they call. And, they don't just win—they become champions."

Blake finished the conversation. "I know you and I were supposed to play a game today, but if it's okay with you, I would like to do that later. I need to 'act decisively' back at the office."

Game Plan

On the way back to the office, Blake called Alex. "Please see if everyone on the leadership team is in the office today. If they are, call a meeting for 2:00." Although Blake believed the business was generally headed in the right direction, he agreed with Jack—they needed more focus on execution.

At 2:00, Blake began. "Thanks for coming on such short notice. I had a good meeting today with Jack, and we talked about the fourth move we need to make to create a high performance organization—Excel at Execution."

"Isn't that what we've been working on?" Charles asked.

"Yes and no," Blake said. "The yes part: we are making good plans and laying the groundwork for the future. The no part: we are not moving with enough urgency. Our conversations have been focused on the first three moves, and we've not done enough to improve our execution. Regardless of what we're working on, we can never forget we must execute. Ultimately, we want to excel in this arena. Right now, we're playing catch-up."

"That's how we lost Sam's business. We took our eye off the ball—we failed to execute," Brad added.

"I agree. Here is what I'd like us to do this afternoon. Let me share some of what I learned today about how we might improve our execution. Then, let's create our action plans for this week."

"What about the other things we've been talking about?" Charles asked. "Are we still going to do those things?"

"What things?" Suzy asked. She was still catching up.

"I'm working on a plan for leadership development, and Brad is working on a communications plan for our vision, mission, and values," Charles responded.

"Yes," Blake interjected. "Certainly. All of that reflects good, critical thinking about our long-term success. We will still do that work. However, if the house is on fire, you don't work on a fire prevention plan."

"You put out the fire," Brad said, finishing Blake's sentence.

"Exactly. We must always be looking for critical gaps; and when we see one, we must attack."

"Attack the gaps—I like that," Angie said.

"How is all this going to be possible? We only have so many hours in a day!" Charles said.

"Granted. That is our reality. That's why this 'chess not checkers' idea makes so much sense to me. Remember, if we do this well, we'll be able to engage the *entire* workforce to help us lead and manage the business. Our success will not be contingent on a few heroic acts by you or me. The more involvement we can create, the more capacity we can generate."

If the house is on fire, you don't work on a fire prevention plan.

"So, that's why we want to Bet on Leadership, Act as One, Win the Heart, and Excel at Execution." Suzy summarized the conversation quite well for someone who had walked into the movie an hour after it started.

"That's a great recap," Blake offered.

"So what do we do?" Brad asked.

"Let me say, it's my fault we have stumbled over the last few months. I apologize. One of my roles, and yours, is to invest enough time on the future of the business to ensure we have one. But at the same time, we cannot become preoccupied with the future at the expense of the present."

"I'm confused," Charles admitted. "I was tracking with you until that last comment. Are we supposed to work on today or tomorrow?"

Suzy jumped in. "Both—that's the leadership challenge Blake is giving us. We have to be concerned with the big picture *and* the details. That's what senior leaders do."

"Thanks, Suzy. You are correct," Blake commented. "That's what I need each of you to do."

"It still sounds hard," Charles added.

"It is! It will be a constant tension that we must manage.

"Let me give you a quick summary of what Jack and I discussed about Excel at Execution. I think it's a timely message for us in light of our current situation."

Blake gave a brief overview of his meeting with Jack.

"So what do we do now?" Angie asked.

Before Blake could respond, Suzy jumped up to the flip chart and said, "Blake wants a plan for the week, and we have already started our long-range planning. Let's recap what's underway and look for gaps."

The team sat in amazement. No one knew Suzy had this in her.

"Okay, Suzy," Angie started. "Here's what I'm working on...."

As she spoke, Suzy wrote her items on the flip chart.

"Who's next?" Suzy asked.

One by one, people shared their work in progress.

After the list was complete, Suzy started at the top and asked two questions: Who is accountable for this? When will it be finished? She then wrote a name and a date by each item. When she finished the last item, she sat down. Looking at Blake, she said, "Is that what you wanted to accomplish today?"

Blake, still surprised by Suzy's adeptness, said, "Yes. Thank you."

"Now," Blake said, as he picked up the facilitation role, "the last step for today—let's look at the list we just made and decide if we are missing anything."

"Attack the gaps," Elizabeth chimed in.

"Exactly," Blake said.

The balance of the conversation uncovered a couple of short-term items the team wanted to do right away. One of them was to have departmental conversations about their individual scorecards. What metrics did each group consider critical, and how could they be monitored? Another item was for Blake to meet with Sam face-to-face. He really didn't expect to get the account back, but he did want to apologize and try to learn as much as possible about why the company lost his business.

"This all makes sense to me," Blake said. "If we believe chess is preferred over checkers, these items should accelerate our journey. Now that we've created our game plan, it's our move."

What's Next?

In the weeks leading up to the planning retreat, a new energy swept the company. The leaders were talking with their team members about what was important and how they might keep score. The ideas generated were diverse—some more creative than others. But all the metrics were effective in letting everyone know the score. They included time to fill a customer's order, accuracy, returns, waste, and overall customer satisfaction. On the Marketing team, Suzy led the group to think beyond sales to the source of sales; they set goals around sales from new customers as well as existing customers. They also decided the size of the order was a good metric to consider. All in all, Blake was pleased. Real, substantive conversations about the business were happening all across the organization.

Blake was also glad he had another meeting with Jack before the retreat. They met in their usual place, and, yes, Jack was playing chess when he arrived.

After the game, Jack said, "Did you make any moves since we last met?"

"Yes, sir," Blake shared several of the items the team was addressing.

"What's next?" Jack asked.

"We are working on our plan to teach the entire organization to play chess not checkers. We're going to introduce our four key moves: Bet on Leadership, Act as One, Win the Heart, and Excel at Execution. Collectively, these have given us a good framework to think about what's next for our business."

"Yes, you can think of these four moves as the blueprint for enrolling everyone on the journey to become a high performance organization," Jack said.

"Then, all we'll need to do is keep learning and growing," Blake added.

"Congratulations," Jack said.

"For what?"

"Your instincts are correct—you must keep pursuing. This idea of high performance is really not something you ever fully realize. Once you think you're finished, you're finished. The competition is not sitting still. If you stop, or sometimes, all you have to do is slow down, the competition will blow right past you. High performance is a lifelong pursuit fueled by personal and organizational learning."

"Well, thanks for your affirmation. Debbie drummed this learning bias into me for several years."

"She was wise to do so," Jack said. "Are you ready to play chess?"

The next hour or so was delightful. Jack was gracious. Rather than annihilating Blake in the first few moves, he talked to him about why he was making each move. He asked questions along the way to prompt Blake to make good decisions. He reminded him to move each piece into positions to leverage its strengths, to involve all his pieces, and to think multiple moves ahead.

Then, all of a sudden, Blake saw something. He looked across the board at Jack.

They both grinned. Blake then took a lone pawn and moved him decisively and said, "Checkmate."

Jack began to clap. "Well done, Blake."

"Either you let me win, or I was extremely lucky," Blake laughed.

"You made the right moves at the right time," Jack said with a wink. "Chess is not a game of luck, and neither is business. When you win, it's because you made good decisions."

"That's what my team and I are trying to do. Thanks for helping us."

"It has been my pleasure."

■ ■ ■

At the retreat, Blake could hardly wait to tell the team he beat Jack in chess.

"I'm excited to spend the next couple of days with you. Before we start, I have some amazing news to share with you: I played Jack in chess last week, and I won! Can you believe it?"

"You must have been really lucky," Charles added.

"I'm glad you mentioned that. I said the same thing to Jack. He corrected me. He said, 'Chess is not a game of luck—neither is business.' He said I won because I made good decisions. And yes, I know he let me win," Blake laughed. "But his point is still valid. We need to make good decisions to win. And, based on what I have seen over the last few months, we've already started.

Chess is not a game of luck, and neither is business. When you win, it's because you made good decisions.

"Before we launch into creating the future, are there any issues we need to discuss about our most recent action items?"

"It's working," Elizabeth said.

"Can you be more specific?" Suzy asked.

"Sure. I mean this whole new way of thinking. I've been challenging my people to think more like making chess moves and not make reactionary jumps like you'd see in checkers. It's made my team stop and think."

"I'll add to that," Brad said. "Just talking to people about how we might keep score has been enlightening. Do you know most of my people were already keeping score?"

"Really?"

"Yeah, the problem is they were all working off different scorecards. They wanted so badly to keep score, they made up their own scorecards—it was very confusing and counterproductive. We are working to resolve that issue."

"How about you, Blake?" Charles asked. "Did you get in to see Sam?"

"Yes, he made me wait three hours in his lobby, but I ultimately got in."

"What did you learn?"

"We blew it—repeatedly. I'm surprised he didn't cut us loose earlier. I listened and apologized. I have also followed up on a few items he mentioned. We need to strengthen our systems to prevent some of those same mistakes from biting us again in the future."

"What's next with Sam?" Suzy asked.

"Nothing as far as I can see. But maybe, just maybe, when we're number one in our industry, he will consider giving us another chance."

Blake continued. "Now, how are we going to become number one? That's the topic of the next few days. My recommendation is to start with our four moves Jack taught us. If done properly, they will help us engage

everyone in the business at a new level. And the truth
is, we won't achieve our goals without them.

"Let's begin by talking about what has already
been done in each area based on our previous meetings and then brainstorm what else we need to do. As
we approach the end of our time, we need to decide
who is going to do what and when." He looked at
Suzy and nodded. She smiled.

"Can I facilitate?" Suzy asked.

"Sure," Blake said.

She went to the front of the room where the team
noticed for the first time there were four flip charts.

"I played a couple of moves ahead and pre-
boarded some things." She flipped a page on each
chart to reveal the words: Bet on Leadership, Act as
One, Win the Heart, and Excel at Execution.

She then opened the floor to a conversation
regarding specific strategies the team could employ
in each area. Many of them were ideas the team had
discussed previously. But there were new ideas, too.

One theme emerged rather quickly: although they
had many talented people on their staff, the team
realized they needed to invest more energy on recruit-
ing and selecting the right people. The days were gone
of filling vacant positions with whoever walked in the
door. High performance organizations don't do that.
Blake challenged the entire leadership team to make
this a key strategy under Act as One. He said, "We
don't need to select people and then find ourselves

trying to *convince* them to embrace our core values. Rather, let's use our values as a litmus test for who we invite to join the organization."

The days were gone of filling vacant positions with whoever walked in the door.

The team also acknowledged the need to build community across the organization. They believed building genuine community would ultimately contribute to their success as a leadership team and would more than likely enhance the engagement of the entire organization as well.

As the process continued, the group was energized as it all began to take shape. Up until that point, they had been working on pieces, not on the whole. Looking at the four moves together made the whole idea come to life and really bolstered their confidence in the approach.

The team knew they were on to something that would require the best leadership of their lives. Chess is more demanding than checkers. They understood that part. What they weren't sure of was how to turn these pages into reality. The team was just sitting there as if staring at a lovely, newly purchased, very large piece of art, captivated by its beauty, and at the same time wondering how they would get it home.

Angie was the first to speak. "I know I have asked this before, but what's next?

"We've got to turn all this into tactical plans and budgets," Brad said as he motioned toward the flip charts.

"That's what I thought," Angie said.

"Any suggestions on how we do that?" Charles asked.

"Maybe I can help with that." The team turned and looked, as a man they didn't know entered the room. "Hi, I'm Jack Deluca. Am I late?"

"No, Jack, you're right on time!" Blake said with a big grin on his face. He and Jack had done their best to keep his participation a secret. Based on the looks on everyone's face, they had succeeded.

Jack shook everyone's hand as they introduced themselves to him.

As everyone took their seat, Jack said, "Blake tells me you are an up-and-coming high performance team. I'm honored to be with you today."

"We're delighted you could join us," Charles said on behalf of the team. "Thanks for all the coaching and encouragement you've provided through your meetings with Blake. We're better because of your investment."

"It's been my pleasure. How can I help today?"

Angie said, "We're just recapping some of our plans to put the four moves into play in our organization."

"I'd love to review those plans with you if you have time," Jack suggested.

"Certainly," Elizabeth said.

The next couple of hours were amazing. As the group reviewed their thought process and their conclusions, Jack pushed the team for clarity on each item—not just what was to be done, but why it was important. It was if they were receiving forty years of wisdom distilled down into a couple of hours.

Finally, Jack said, "When I came in, I believe you were asking how to translate these strategies into specific tactics. Is that correct?"

"Yes," Suzy said, "that was the question."

Jack said, "I have a suggestion, but before I offer it, I want to share a thought with you. Perhaps this is intuitively obvious, but I want to tell you *why* the four moves—Bet on Leadership, Act as One, Win the Heart, and Excel at Execution—are important. Have you considered that question?"

The group just sat there, not sure if that was a rhetorical question or not.

Blake spoke up and said, "We've talked about the individual moves, but I've probably not talked enough about why the moves matter collectively."

"It's simple, actually. In chess, the more pieces you involve in the game, the greater your chances of winning; in business, including more people has the same effect. People want to be valued; they want to be useful; they want to contribute. When you make the moves we've been talking about, people show up in a whole new way. It changes everything—their engagement skyrockets. As a result, the people and the organization are transformed. Some call it a high performance organization; I call it remarkable. The untapped potential of people always amazes me."

In chess, the more pieces you involve in the game, the greater your chances of winning.

Everyone nodded in agreement. It was clear: they were still processing what they had just heard from Jack. It was a defining moment for the team. Previously, they had been focused on *what* to do; Jack had just helped them understand the bigger *why*.

After a moment of silence, Jack continued. "So, my suggestion is for you to always look for meaningful ways to involve your people in the work. In this case, I would recommend each team take thirty days to get input from your people and then complete your plans. You can then bring your work back to this group for input and approval."

Blake said, "Let's do that—everyone has thirty days to get input from your team members."

"Jack, thank you for joining us today. It was a tremendous gift to our team. Can you stay for dinner?" Elizabeth asked.

"Yes, I think I can."

"Outstanding!" Blake said. "We're adjourned."

■ ■ ■

Unfortunately, Jack could not be with the team on day 2 of the retreat, but his appearance on day 1 left an unmistakable imprint on the energy and enthusiasm of the entire team.

The next day, both Charles and Elizabeth presented great ideas to help the organization play chess not checkers. Several of their suggestions were adopted for implementation across the organization. One tactic Blake especially liked was a quarterly meeting with the entire company. He would use the first of these gatherings to share the purpose, mission, and values for the first time. The leadership team would then assist with communications after Blake's first public presentation. Blake had shared Jack's challenge about cascading key messages with the team—this would be an ongoing focus. They all knew to successfully Act as One would require each of them to constantly communicate with their team members.

On the issue of Bet on Leadership, Charles recommended every leader identify someone for targeted development who might someday be his or her replacement. Suzy made sure each action item had a specific owner and a clear deadline. She was incredible!

As the retreat neared its end, Blake went around the room and talked about the unique contribution of each member of the team. He thanked them personally for sharing their strengths and passions with the company. He saved Suzy for last.

"Suzy, thank you for your patience with me, Boss #5. You could have easily walked away at any point over the years. I'm glad you stayed. Thanks, too, for helping me navigate those early days. You knew I was in over my head, but you never said anything about it. Thanks, also, for the way you have stepped up in Marketing. The team has responded to your leadership extremely well. And, finally, thanks for all you have done in your short tenure on this team. You are really making a difference! If you're willing, I would like to remove the interim from your title and officially offer you the job, Vice President of Marketing."

Everyone clapped.

"Thank you," Suzy said. "I don't think I've done anything special; I'm just trying to play chess not checkers—right?"

Everyone laughed.

"Right," Blake said. "That's all there is to it."

■ ■ ■

When Blake got home, Megan met him at the door.

"How was it?"

"Really good. How are the kids?"

"They're fine. They'd love to spend more time with their hero."

"I know. I think we are about to get a handle on this thing. My plan is to spend a lot more time with you and the kids in the weeks and months to come."

"I hope so," Megan said as she hugged Blake. "Tell me what happened. How are you feeling?"

"I'm thankful for the opportunity to lead this business. I'm thankful for the team. I'm thankful you didn't tell me I wasn't ready to be a CEO. I'm thankful to have Debbie in my life—I need to send her some flowers. I'm thankful to have Jack as my mentor. And, finally, I'm thankful to know that leading a high performance organization is all about chess not checkers! We are making real progress, and it feels great!"

Megan was beaming as she listened to Blake's summary. "Your dad was right, and I knew it all along: you are becoming a great leader."

Epilogue

The next six months were crazy, frustrating, exhilarating days for Blake and the team. There was so much to do that the team ultimately decided they needed to scale back the plan for the upcoming year. They didn't abandon any of the moves; they just decided to implement their plan a little more slowly—"narrow the focus," as Jack would say. This made the implementation of their ideas much easier.

Performance continued to improve. In retrospect, it made perfect sense—if you invest in your leadership; ensure the entire organization understands your purpose, mission, and values; leverage people's strengths and help them pursue their dreams; and create systems to enable great performance. It works!

The most frustrating part of the entire journey was the realization some of their employees didn't want to play chess—they were more than happy with checkers. Those people had to go.

As the company grew stronger and stronger, its reputation and market share grew as well. So much so, Blake was surprised to get an email from Sam, the client they had lost almost a year earlier. It said, "Call me." Blake did and that call led to a visit, and that visit led to a restored relationship. Blake and the team had their biggest client back.

Suzy thrived in her new role. She became the poster child for pursuing your passions. Her story was told over and over and became an inspiration to countless employees.

Blake continued to meet with Jack. When he did, they talked about business and played chess. Blake never beat Jack again, but with every visit he became a better leader.

At home, Megan was delighted Blake was making progress at work. Their quality of life improved steadily over the months. Blake was even able to be home for dinner with amazing regularity—the kids loved getting their dad back.

Finally, perhaps the best part of the entire turnaround scenario was Blake's newfound confidence in himself and others. As he discovered, chess not checkers was more than a way to think, and Jack's four moves were more than a blueprint for high performance; these were ideas capable of unlocking an entire new world of possibility for his people, his organization, and himself.

Blake's next challenge: How would he honor his agreement with Jack and pay it forward? He had some ideas. . . .

Acknowledgments

If you have never written a book, let me share a secret with you: it requires dozens, if not hundreds, of people to make a project like this a reality. Although it is impossible to publically acknowledge everyone who contributed to this effort, I want to recognize some of them here.

To begin, I want to thank the people who helped create the core content: Jeff Steggert, Scott Wozniak, and Betsy Zint played indispensable roles in the process of bringing this book to life. Their research, insight, creativity, and dedication to the work, combined with their patience with me, were remarkable. Their diligence during this project enabled us to find a realistic and proven path to high performance. That was the first domino that had to fall, or this book would not exist. Thank you!

Thanks to the following business leaders who provided working laboratories in which we could identify and validate the ideas outlined in this book: Ryan Allen, Paul Becker, Chris Beckler, William Boulware, Bryan Bullington, Roger Clark, John Collette, Mandy Cooper, Kurt Davis, Joseph DeCola, Ryan

Dennis, Glen Efford, Scott Fraser, Jamie Fuller, Bob Garrett, Natasha Gilbert, Quart Graves, Michael Hancock, Joe Hatzopoulos, Robert Hensen, John Hughes, Duane Johnston, Gary Kasprzak, Greg Kubala, Brad Lingerfelt, Mike Ludwig, Frieda Marroquin, Matt Michaels, John Moore, Mike Moore, Rob Morris, Bart Norman, Cliff Parker, Greg Patterson, Daniel Perry, Becky Pickle, Joseph Piotrowski, Lauren Plain, Jonathan Purser, Dusty Pyne, Gene Robinson, Rob Rogers, Dean Sandbo, Craig Saxton, Josh Sells, Chug Shafe, Kendrick Skipper, Bruce Slone, Dan Stanko, Rick Starkweather, Art TerKeurst, Shane Todd, KJ Wari, Matt Webber, Joe Weber, Erich Weiss, Luke Wilbanks, Brad Williams, and Cindy Wilson.

Thanks also to the team that commissioned this work years ago. Tim Tassopoulos, Andrew Cathy, Dee Ann Turner, Cliff Robinson, and Rob Dugas saw the need for this project. Their instincts were correct: High performance is not a matter of circumstances, luck, or DNA. High performance is about choices—just like chess. Thanks for your vision and your leadership.

Thanks to my wife Donna and to my friends Randy Gravitt and Mark Conklin, who joined the outstanding editorial team at Berrett-Koehler to edit and polish this manuscript. Their efforts added tremendous value—in both content and style.

And, finally, as noted earlier, this book is dedicated to Truett Cathy. Chick-fil-A is not a perfect organization. However, Truett understood the key to long-term success is much more about chess than it is checkers. I'm thankful he showed me, and the world, how to play the game exceedingly well.

About the Author

Mark Miller is a business leader, best-selling author, and communicator.

Mark began writing about a decade ago. He teamed up with Ken Blanchard, coauthor of *The One Minute Manager*, to write *The Secret: What Great Leaders Know and Do*. Today, over half a million copies of *The Secret* are in print, and it has been translated into more than twenty-five languages. Recently, he released *The Secret of Teams*, which outlines key lessons learned from a twenty-year exploration of the question "Why do some teams outperform the rest?" His most recent book, *The Heart of Leadership*, released in March 2014, explores how to become the type of leader people want to follow.

In addition to his writing, Mark loves speaking to leaders. Over the years, he's traveled extensively around the world teaching for numerous international organizations. His theme is always the same:

encouraging and equipping leaders. His topics include leadership, creativity, team building, and more. Mark started his Chick-fil-A career working as an hourly team member in 1977. In 1978, he joined the corporate staff working in the warehouse and mailroom. Since that time, he has provided leadership for Corporate Communications, Field Operations, Quality and Customer Satisfaction, Training and Development, and Organizational Effectiveness. Today, he serves as the Vice President for Leadership Development. During his years with Chick-fil-A, annual sales have grown to over $5 billion. The company has almost two thousand restaurants in thirty-nine states and the District of Columbia.

Mark lives an active lifestyle. As a photographer, he's enjoyed shooting in some of the world's hardest-to-reach places, including Antarctica, Everest Base Camp, the jungles of Rwanda, and the Galápagos Islands.

Mark is also active in social media. He'd love to connect with you:

Website: **GreatLeadersServe.com**
Twitter: **@LeadersServe**
Facebook: **Great Leaders Serve**
Linkedin: **Mark Miller**

Additional Resources

If you've found value in the ideas contained in *Chess Not Checkers*, you may be interested in the following resources.

CHESS NOT CHECKERS
Organizational Assessment

If you want to create a high performance organization, which of the four moves should you focus on first? Are there gaps between leadership's perception of reality and the front-line workers' point of view? Where are your blind spots?

The Chess Not Checkers Organizational Assessment has been created to help you find the answers to these questions and more!

Here's how it works:

Go to *GreatLeaderServe.com* to purchase the assessment. Once downloaded, have as many people in your organization as possible complete the anonymous, online survey—the higher the participation rate, the more accurate your results.

After your organization has completed the assessment, you'll receive a detailed report showing your areas of strength and opportunities for improvement, including specific recommendations.

CHESS NOT CHECKERS
Field Guide

This guide was created as a companion to this book and contains practical ideas to help you create your own high performance organization.

The field guide is appropriate for group or individual study. Each guide contains group exercises and an answer key. You can purchase the field guide at *GreatLeadersServe.com*. Quantity discounts are available.

CHESS NOT CHECKERS
Video Series

Join your host, Randy Gravitt, on a guided tour to explore the four moves Blake learned from Jack in *Chess Not Checkers*.

Randy will take you through the content of the *Chess Not Checkers Field Guide* chapter by chapter. (The videos were produced so you can use them without the field guide if you would like.) This video series contains more than a dozen sessions full of practical examples and group exercises.

To see a sample of the videos or make a purchase, go to *GreatLeadersServe.com/resources*.

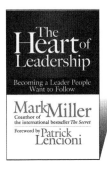
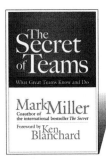

With Ken Blanchard

The Secret
What Great Leaders Know and Do, Third Edition

Join struggling young executive Debbie
Brewster as she explores a profound yet
seemingly contradictory concept: to lead
is to serve. Along the way she learns why
great leaders seem preoccupied with the
future, what three arenas require con-
tinuous improvement, the two essential
components to leadership success, how
to knowingly strengthen—or unwittingly
destroy—leadership credibility, and more.

Hardcover, 144 pages, ISBN 978-1-62656-198-4
PDF ebook, ISBN 978-1-62656-199-1

Great Leaders Grow
Becoming a Leader for Life

What is the key ingredient for a long-term,
high-impact career in leadership? Debbie
Brewster tells Blake Brown, her late mentor's son, "Your capacity to grow determines
your capacity to lead" and helps Blake discover and apply four strategies for personal
growth. These same strategies can enhance
your life and leadership too! Join Blake and
explore the path to increased leadership
effectiveness and influence.

Hardcover, 144 pages, ISBN 978-1-60994-303-5
PDF ebook, ISBN 978-1-60509-695-7

BK Berrett–Koehler Publishers, Inc.
    www.bkconnection.com   **800.929.2929**

Berrett–Koehler
Publishers

Berrett-Koehler is an independent publisher dedicated to an ambitious mission: *Connecting people and ideas to create a world that works for all.*

Our publications span many formats, including print, digital, audio, and video. We also offer online resources, training, and gatherings. And we will continue expanding our products and services to advance our mission.

We believe that the solutions to the world's problems will come from all of us, working at all levels: in our society, in our organizations, and in our own lives. Our publications and resources offer pathways to creating a more just, equitable, and sustainable society. They help people make their organizations more humane, democratic, diverse, and effective (and we don't think there's any contradiction there). And they guide people in creating positive change in their own lives and aligning their personal practices with their aspirations for a better world.

And we strive to practice what we preach through what we call "The BK Way." At the core of this approach is *stewardship,* a deep sense of responsibility to administer the company for the benefit of all of our stakeholder groups, including authors, customers, employees, investors, service providers, sales partners, and the communities and environment around us. Everything we do is built around stewardship and our other core values of *quality, partnership, inclusion,* and *sustainability.*

This is why Berrett-Koehler is the first book publishing company to be both a B Corporation (a rigorous certification) and a benefit corporation (a for-profit legal status), which together require us to adhere to the highest standards for corporate, social, and environmental performance. And it is why we have instituted many pioneering practices (which you can learn about at www.bkconnection.com), including the Berrett-Koehler Constitution, the Bill of Rights and Responsibilities for BK Authors, and our unique Author Days.

We are grateful to our readers, authors, and other friends who are supporting our mission. We ask you to share with us examples of how BK publications and resources are making a difference in your lives, organizations, and communities at www.bkconnection.com/impact.

Dear reader,

Thank you for picking up this book and welcome to the worldwide BK community! You're joining a special group of people who have come together to create positive change in their lives, organizations, and communities.

What's BK all about?

Our mission is to connect people and ideas to create a world that works for all.

Why? Our communities, organizations, and lives get bogged down by old paradigms of self-interest, exclusion, hierarchy, and privilege. But we believe that can change. That's why we seek the leading experts on these challenges—and share their actionable ideas with you.

A welcome gift

To help you get started, we'd like to offer you a **free copy** of one of our bestselling ebooks:

www.bkconnection.com/welcome

When you claim your **free ebook**, you'll also be subscribed to our blog.

Our freshest insights

Access the best new tools and ideas for leaders at all levels on our blog at ideas.bkconnection.com.

Sincerely,

Your friends at Berrett-Koehler